MW00767914

RECONSTRUCTION

Defying Cancer and Building a More Purposeful Life

Melissa A. Powell Weaver

Can someone truly change in less than one minute? The answer is yes, but the real questions are how will you change and what will it look like? In August of 2013, I was told that I had an aggressive form of breast cancer. In less than one minute my life was forever transformed, but not in the ways you might think. I lost many things during my battle with cancer, but I gained even more. Ever since that fateful day, I have made it my mission to inspire others to not just survive trauma but to learn to recreate, reprioritize, and refocus their lives. We make choices every day that continuously influence our existence but the question remains, are we making the right decisions, the ones that ultimately create a life worth living?

© 2016 Melissa A. Powell Weaver. All rights reserved.
No part of this publication may be produced or transmitted in any form or by any means. This includes mechanical, photocopying, electronic, and recording. This also includes any information obtained via storage or retrieval systems. Written permission from the author must be granted prior to use, in any form, of the book including all contents. A reviewer, who may use direct quotes, photos, and/or video material for reviewing purposes only, can use the material contained in the book.

Disclaimer: The following story and information should not be used to diagnose or treat any illness including a mental health diagnosis. Furthermore, the material is not suitable for every situation. The work is bought and sold with the explicit understanding that the Author and reader **have not** engaged in any form of a professionally therapeutic relationship and neither the Author nor the Publisher shall be held liable for damages arising here from. In the event that an organization, book, movie, or website is referred to in this work, it does not mean that the Author endorses the information that the organization, book, movie, or website may provide or recommend. Finally, readers should be aware that information contained in this book related to illness and treatment is the opinion and personal experience of the Author, and **should not** be considered medical advice or treatment.

Cover Design: Robin Baxter
Book Cover Photographer: Beth Oliver
Editing: Jennifer Warren & Kirsten Vroman
Formatting: Linda Parlove
Book Promotions: Tracey & Blaise Wingold
Photography: Chrystie Varn
Special thanks to Suzi, Juliet and Isabel Weaver

*For my amazing wife and children
who have taught me the art of love.*

TABLE OF CONTENTS

For the Luck of Cancer

If you were to see the scars that rest on my now flattened chest you might not consider me lucky, but you are not looking deep enough.

If you were to watch me climb out of bed each morning stiff from the medicine that continues to keep the stalker at bay you would not consider me lucky, but you are still not looking deep enough.

If you were to sit with me as I wait for the next scan that could determine whether I will see my children grow you would not consider me lucky, but you have yet to see the miracle that has occurred.

Before cancer I raced through life running towards an invisible finish line. I often neglected to stop and look at the change in scenery, the changes in my children's faces, or the amazing beauty this life as to offer.

Before cancer I would often put work before family, obligations before fun, and daily life before living. Before cancer I was in a dark room with only a flashlight to see the things that surrounded me.

Cancer has flooded my once dark room with light.

I can now see all of the beauty that encompasses my life.

I see my children snuggled close beside me, telling me of their dreams.

I can see my beautiful partner whom I barely knew these last thirteen years.

I can see that quiet meditation calms my once racing mind.

I was lost before cancer, floating through life like the last leaf falling from a barren tree. I found myself in cancer, and found that luck is something that surrounds you every day - you just have to turn the lights on!

–Melissa Powell Weaver

PREFACE

When did I decide that my life was worth saving? I think the moment I made this crucial decision was after a long and painful deconstruction of the hidden spaces where I had carefully concealed years of guilt, pain, and self-loathing. Cancer might have destroyed a part of me, but it also gave birth to the person I am today. I did not arrive at this new state easily. There were battles lost along the way. But the beaten, fragmented, and war-torn pieces that remained began to take hold. Over the last two years, through the desolate, cracked pieces of my soul, a new life has emerged.

Can we really reconstruct our lives following great devastation? If so, then how do we get there? I am living proof that the answer to the first question is yes: we can rebuild. Although there may be roadblocks on the path to recovery, we alone have the ability not only to repair, but to create healthier versions of the people we once were. By taking a brave step towards personal growth we ultimately cause a ripple effect of inspiration, motivation, and transformation.

Although this book is a personal story about my journey with breast cancer, it has been carefully and thoughtfully written for anyone who has been knocked over by tragedy or loss and is desperately searching for solid ground on which to rebuild. Think of this book as a lifeline to your best self, the part that clings to the life that you were always supposed to lead, valuing what and who truly matters most to you. As you move through this true story, know that I have designed the text so that you will easily be able to absorb and act on these essential life secrets. Right now you may be saying to yourself, "I can wait to read this next year." I strongly encourage you to fight the urge to put this invaluable information on hold, as it is not only life changing but also potentially life saving.

A Licensed Clinical Social Worker by trade, I have worked with many individuals and organizations that talk of change. I have spent countless hours in meetings specifically focused on reorganizing and restructuring one's business, life, or priorities. But the question remains: how many individuals or organizations actually make change happen? If this change does occur, can it be successfully maintained?

Through a difficult, uncertain, and fearful journey I have emerged a stronger, more engaged, and determined individual. This in no way means that I don't experience moments of failure, fear, and disappointment. But despite the fact that my future is entirely unclear and my time on this earth is uncertain, I choose to continue to be an active and committed player in my life and the lives of others. There are days when I don't want to get out of bed, and there are moments where fear temporarily causes a sense of emotional paralysis. When this happens I fight through the feelings, find I am stronger than I thought I was, and I am the hero in my own story.

Stop and ask yourself what lead you to this book: "What am I searching for? How do I take the first step to find it?" You have already taken the first step, and I will show you the way to a stronger and happier version of yourself. With your commitment and focus, you too, can stand in the sun. Do not wait for another year, hour, minute, or second to pass you by. Do not allow time and happiness to slip through your fingertips. Now is the time to take control of your life and say to yourself: "I can be the change."

Inside the pages of this book you will find some of my deepest and most private thoughts, struggles, and secrets to letting go of cancer and taking back my life. You might be wondering: why I am choosing to share these thoughts, feelings, and strategies. The answer is simple - I want to inspire others to not just live, but live a life that they can be proud of. I want others to know of the freedom that comes from releasing what we think that we know about our happiness, our priorities, and ourselves, and learning that we can truly be, have, and do so much more with our lives. My goal is for this book to become something that you refer back to throughout your life at times when you are looking for something to keep you grounded, focused, or committed. This book will be life changing but only if you are ready, and more importantly, willing to BE THE CHANGE!

CHAPTER 1
The Spark

Online Health Journal Entry

Lost and Found
Sep 7, 2013 11:03pm

So one week and four days ago, on August 29th, I was told that I had breast cancer. Since then it has been an emotional roller coaster. I have really terrible moments and some when I actually forget that I have cancer. Surprisingly enough I have learned so many things over this very long week. The first thing that I have learned is that I have the most amazing friends and family. I truly do not think that I could have made it through these days without my amazing support system. I hit what I am hoping to be rock bottom yesterday; today I actually belly laughed for the first time since I first learned of the diagnosis. My standards for cleaning have been greatly reduced, and I have learned that when a vegetable smoothie calls for arugula it actually only means a couple of pieces and not ten. Wow! That was the worst smoothie that I have ever had. I am truly trying to find the inner peace within myself and accept the things that I cannot control, but who am I kidding - that completely goes against my DNA makeup. I guess all that I can do is take things one day, hour, or minute at a time.

Love to all,
M

Is there a moment when you knew your life would be forever changed? It is an undeniable fact that I am broken, deformed, and scarred, but this is only a part of me and not at all the best part. I am a wife, mother, daughter, sister, friend, and most importantly a survivor. Cancer does not define who I am or who I will become, but it is a solidified part of my journey. This is my own true story, but it is a story I share with so many others just like me who have learned to let go of tragedy and take back their lives.

I could feel the panic well up inside of me and knew that if I were to truly succumb to it, I ultimately would be taken to a place of no return. As I sat in the dark, a piece of me was still connected to this world, but most was residing in a place of irrational thoughts and actions. This surreal experience occurred three days after learning of my cancer diagnosis. Although I wish that I could say it was the thing that ultimately changed my life, it was just the spark.

I've been told that I was in love with life from the moment I entered the world. My mother often describes a child who rarely stopped smiling and who loved exploring all that life had to offer. As the years passed, fear and self-doubt slowly took over, and the girl I once knew eventually disappeared.
It would take many years and a life threatening illness to uncover the individual buried so deep. Looking back now, I wonder why it took almost twenty years to find this person again? How did I spend so many years caged by self-doubt, anxiety, and fear of rejection? Was cancer some foreign entity that unknowingly entered and reeked havoc on my mind and body or was it always there disguised as anxiety and insecurity? I believe that my illness was the result of many culminated components that eventually made up the perfect storm.

I learned early in life how to run, but it would take me twenty years to realize what I actually was running from. I joined track and cross country teams at an early age and was an accomplished athlete by the time I got to high school. At the same time, I also was running an emotionally uphill race from the start. Anxiety, depression, and alcoholism were genetic staples in our family, and I was continuously vulnerable to their potential effects. However, I like to think that my inherited traits of determination, compassion, and kindness were those that ultimately shaped the person I am today.

My father was a larger than life figure in the community I grew up in, and when he gave love, it was strong love. Although he possessed the ability to inspire, lead, and engage others, he experienced rapid shifts in mood. Unfortunately, these emotionally challenging times would initiate a sense of uncertainty and ultimately impact my personal growth. That having been said, my mother was, and still is, the most consistent, rational, and unshakable individual I know. Ultimately, it would be her ability to overcome great adversity that would keep our family intact and grounded; a skill she would use again almost twenty years later when I was diagnosed with cancer.

I spent most of my life wanting so much to please my father, aspiring to be everything that he needed and expected; but I often felt as though I had let him down. I believe that this unrealized need would fuel my great desire for approval from others and lead to many years of failed relationships. Instead of spending my young adult life discovering my true identity, I would look to others to provide for my sense of purpose.

Despite our often-tumultuous relationship, I learned many things from my father. I remember all too well the early morning or weekend training sessions, when time after time my father stretched me to my limits in his determined attempts to create a competitive runner. It would only be many years later, during my cancer treatment, that I would smile, as I finally realized that what he was (unknowingly) giving me was the precious gift of life-saving endurance.

I will never forget the last race my father ever saw me run. It was the state championship cross-country meet, and true to his form, my father came with both a stopwatch and the desire for victory. I can still feel the cold and damp weather, and can vividly sense my legs tremble as they pushed through the mud and over the steep terrain. I wanted to stop so badly. I was cold and in pain, but I heard my father yelling. His words of encouragement and my intense desire for his approval drove me onward. As I crested the hill and began my sprint towards the finish line, I noticed that I was picking up speed and that I would, in fact, break my personal record. Not until many years later did my mother tell me the story of how, in his excited moment of sheer joy, my father dropped his camera, leaving the only documentation of the race in my mind.

I was sixteen years old when symptoms of panic and anxiety first occurred. My life was turned upside down and all that I knew to be certain was gone. As it is with many fathers and daughters, our relationship began experiencing significant growing pains during my teenage years. Since this was common in families, we both expected that as time progressed, so would our relationship. Unfortunately, my father and I did not have time. He died at age forty-seven of a brain aneurism. The loss of my father left not only a gap in my life, but set the stage for a deep-seated fear of my own early death, and later, a basic instinct to protect my own children from experiencing the death of a young parent. I was sixteen when my father passed away. Although the details are now hazy, I vividly remember falling to my knees in shock and grief as I received the devastating news. With my father's untimely death came my first real experience of personal trauma...and growth. I learned through it that grief weighs heavily on the heart and can create deep and gaping wounds. My primal reaction of despair and disbelief repeated itself years later after learning of my cancer diagnosis at age thirty-seven.

It took me years to overcome the loss of my father, and not for the reasons one might suspect. Because of my mother's complete dedication to fostering a sense of normalcy and healing for my sisters and me, I was able to develop a life without this hugely influential person - my other parent. However, my loss would trigger uncertainties about my own life, health, and self-identity, and I would spend the next twenty years putting the puzzle pieces back together - just in time to have them come crashing down again.

With my father's passing went the possibility of a stronger, healthier, and reconstructed relationship. Following this loss, I began what I refer to as "my continual fall from sanity." Due, at least in part, to my somewhat tumultuous relationship with my father, I entered my teens with a distinct lack of self-identity. The wounds created during these formative years were deep and would continue to weep and fester until well into my twenties.

Three words describe this time as a young adult: I WAS LOST! During this time, I wish I could say that I did something redeeming and noteworthy, like saving the planet or the human race at large, but my contributions to society would not come until much later in life. I spent the better part of my young adult years further losing myself in mostly self-induced toxic relationships, searching for the next method of escape, and thinking that I would have unlimited time to fix what was broken. I know that my story is like many other tales of young adulthood, but what I would learn almost twenty years later, was that forever can come to an end much sooner than we're prepared for.

I'm not proud of the person I was in my early adult years. I didn't take the time to look inside myself for answers, but instead looked to others for a validation and love. I spent a great deal of energy and time moving from one place (or relationship) to the next, all in an attempt to discover my purpose and place in life. What I didn't realize at the time was, I could have been so much more had I just stayed still. Of course, I know that if I could do it all again I would choose differently, but regret is often at the core of self-loathing and insecurity. Therefore, I choose to see that experience as a time of great learning and a representation of the person I needed to leave behind.

Faced with the long journey into adulthood, I was also plagued with a sense that I was somehow different than everyone else. Although being a good athlete, student, and daughter was my focus, I carried around a constant belief that I was incapable of receiving love. Eventually, I came to learn that the absence of self-acceptance of who I was *supposed* to be was at the core of my internal chaos.

The truth was, and still is, that who I'm *supposed* to be is an ever-evolving process. When I came to realize and acknowledge that I was a lesbian, it became just one of the many stops along my lifelong journey of self-exploration. Unfortunately, I had to wait several years, blindly navigating through the world of young love to find what I was searching for. Discovering true love of self and others meant letting go of the only life I knew.

RECONSTRUCTION

CHAPTER 2
The Flame and the Fire

Online Health Journal Entry

I am Blessed
Sep 14, 2013 1:40pm

I have cancer and I feel blessed. There are few times in one's life where the words blessed and cancer are used simultaneously, but this is one of those times. I have been told that when a person is given a cancer diagnosis it is normal to experience feelings of anger, despair, and utter terror; and although I have had all of these feelings and many more, I never expected the words blessed and lucky to be a part of my current vocabulary. I feel blessed for: the new pace of my day to day life, the sun on my face; the unbelievably amazing faith of the village that has surrounded me, and the loving family that grounds me during a time when I feel as though I could easily lose my footing. There are times that I still feel terrified and lost; however, knowing that I have so many amazing and wonderful people and circumstances surrounding me gives me the strength to face another day.

Love to All
M

RECONSTRUCTION

Love can come in slowly with gentle hands, or it can slam into us leaving our world turned upside down. An unexpected relationship in my early twenties opened up a world of authenticity and emotion I had never felt. Initially, I attributed this feeling to friendship, but it would later prove to be the match that ignited a flame I couldn't put out. After letting go of the life I thought I would lead as a heterosexual woman, I began to break free from the chains that bound me to a life I could never fully embrace, so I could instead feel the freedom to spread my wings and fly. This relationship was short-lived, but through it, I found I could no longer deny the person I was or was going to become.

My wife, Suzi, came into my life following a time of emotional exploration. Our love was not instantaneous, but instead would slowly infiltrate each fiber of my being; creating in me a sense of permanence and stability that had not previously existed. With Suzi came the emotional structure and responsibility I believe I needed but wasn't emotionally strong enough to fully embrace at that time. In my relationship with Suzi, I first learned not only how receive love, but also how to carefully nurture the fragile gift I had been given. My connection with her was like a fire that warms the soul on the coldest of days and continues to burn long after the flame. On a rainy, warm day in August, on a beautiful beach surrounded by close family and friends, I peacefully and confidently walked down a sandy aisle to marry the person I had waited my whole life for, and said the words: "You made me want to be a better person."

Until I decided to commit myself to Suzi, I had lacked clarity and consistency in my emotional connections; however, my professional path was clear and steadfast from the beginning. Around the time I entered middle school I knew I wanted to be a social worker, a career I learned from my mother. As a young adult, I spent hours thinking about the inequities of life, concepts of compassion, and empathy. The possibility of giving back provided for a sense of inspiration and hope. I realized very quickly that I was drawn to those in need, individuals who had experienced great tragedy and loss. Although the idea of helping others was crucial, I also wanted to inspire others to become more resilient, so that in the end, they could become the heroes of their own stories. After completing my undergraduate degree at Virginia Commonwealth University, I landed a job as a social worker at a local rehabilitation facility where I worked closely with individuals facing significant health challenges. Although I had to work two jobs to make ends meet, the work provided for a sense of empowerment, giving back, and was something that I truly loved. After many years in the healthcare setting, I decided I would return to school in order to earn my Master's degree in social work, and to eventually become a hospice social worker. However, my plan for professional growth would soon take a back seat to what life had in store for me next.

Suzi and I knew early in our relationship that we wanted to have a family, but we weren't prepared for the unimaginable love we would feel for our future daughters. We would ultimately learn through this journey of parenthood that a family is what you make of it, and that love is not dependent on the approval of others or biological connections. Once we decided to have children, we talked about how we both wanted to carry a child. Because Suzi is eight years older than me, we agreed she would become pregnant first. Searching for just the right anonymous donor was fairly similar to searching an online dating service. We asked ourselves: "Do we want someone tall or short? With blonde hair or brown? Should they be good at sports or a lover of the arts?" We quickly learned the differences between fertility and online dating websites. First, we received more random details about our potential donor than most individuals know about their spouses after a lifetime of marriage. Second, we totally avoided all of the potential cyber stalking incidents that occur with online dating! All joking aside, Suzi and I combed through hundreds of potential donors until we settled on a brown-haired, blue-eyed man, who had great exposure to the arts and was, most importantly, the perfect mix of the two of us. On March 23, 2006, our daughter Juliet was born. I will admit I felt a little lost in this new role of mother, and I desperately yearned to fully embrace it. Since Suzi was nursing Juliet, I had to find a way to develop my own special bond with her. My search wouldn't take long. When Juliet was almost three months old, Suzi decided to return to work. She loved our child very much, but knew that she needed to be back in the workforce. After much discussion, we decided that I would stay at home with our beautiful new daughter. At first I was timid and doubtful I could care for this amazing creation, but a forced lesson in parenthood quickly proved that I was, in fact, her mother. With it came all of the happiness, anxiety, and tearfulness of parenthood.

One warm summer's day, I was giving Juliet some medicine. She began to cough in a way that hadn't happened before, and I, being a new parent, began to panic, as I feared that she was choking. I quickly ran through possible options in my mind: go to find help, dial 911, attempt CPR! As I began to cry and beg her to be alright (as if my pleas would somehow magically fix the problem,) she let out a huge cry! I knew then that she would be just fine. At that very moment, a love like I had never known washed over me, and I instantly realized it was a forever kind of love - the bond between us as mother and child was solidified.

When our beautiful Juliet turned one, Suzi and I decided it was time to have a second child, so we ventured into a journey that would bring heartache, and ultimately, a small spirited miracle. Because of infertility complications, I needed hormonal treatment in order to conceive a child. In the early fall of 2007, we were thrilled to learn that I was pregnant. I felt instantly connected to the beautiful life growing inside my belly, and spent time planning for this new arrival. However, we were soon subjected to one of the cruelest of all circumstances, the loss of a child.

It was a mild winter's day, days before the holiday season. I was at my part-time job while Juliet was with her Grandmother, and as I was in the restroom, I noticed the first signs of blood. I immediately contacted my doctor's office who told me to come in to make sure everything was okay. To say that I was panicked is an understatement, but I kept telling myself that I had to hold it together for my child. I drove myself to the doctor's office where Suzi was waiting. As the doctor performed the ultrasound, he looked at us with a sigh of relief saying that he wasn't quite sure what caused the bleeding, but that the baby was just fine. I was in complete disbelief, but so very happy. He again provided reassurance by letting us hear and see our baby's heartbeat. As I walked out of the office, still shaken, I felt so very grateful and full of hope.

We enjoyed a wonderful holiday, filled with gratitude for our beautiful toddler and upcoming new addition. Since all was well with our unborn baby, Suzi and I decided that we would make our annual out-of-town visit to our friend's home for New Years. We had a wonderful visit down south, but I began experiencing overwhelming emotions of fear and sadness. I eventually dismissed them as continued jitters related to the recent scare and hormonal changes, and decided I would focus my attention and efforts on the upcoming doctor's appointment where we would get another look at our beautiful child.

I was very nervous as we walked into the OB/GYN's office on January 3rd, and, although I couldn't find the exact cause, I had overwhelming feelings of doom and loss. During the ultrasound I closely observed the face of the female technician, anxious to discover any changes in her expression. When she finally stood up, without making eye contact, she said that she'd be right back. I instinctively knew that something wasn't right and was intensely afraid of what would happen next. After what seemed like an eternity, the OB/GYN came into the room and had the technician perform the ultrasound again. Once it was completed, the doctor sat down beside me and, in a calm and quiet tone said, "I am so sorry, but we could not locate a heartbeat." For a moment, I wasn't certain whether she meant the baby's or mine. I was positive that on that cold day in January my heart stopped beating. As we left the office and realized that at sixteen weeks pregnant we had lost our child, I had the feeling that time was standing still and that darkness was closing in. I would later relive those same emotions on a warm day in August 2013.

The doctor told me that I could go home and have a glass of wine to take the edge off, but I couldn't drink alcohol, as part of me held out hope that this was all a mistake, and that my child was still alive in my body. As I took a shower that night, I cried tears that came from the most primal place in my soul. I mourned the fact that I could not will my body to save this child, and I told my beautiful baby that I would never let them go. Unfortunately, this was not the last time my body would betray me and take something from me that I held so dear. But during both of these times of loss and grief, I would find a way to stand up and take back my life. After the recommended waiting period, we decided it was time to try again for our second child, and so the story of Isabel began.

Isabel was a fighter from the very start. During the first six weeks of this pregnancy, I once again experienced bleeding, but this spirited little girl was determined she would make her entrance into this world. Was it ever an entrance! At thirty weeks I began experiencing contractions, and because of the loss of one baby, I was understandably scared and anxious. Then during the thirty-seventh week I stopped feeling Isabel move. Determined that my daughter would live, I quickly reached out to the OB/GYN. I was admitted to the hospital and the birthing process of our daughter began.

My goal was to have a natural childbirth, but life has a way of changing our paths, and Isabel's birth was no exception. After many hours of trying to induce labor, the nurses and doctors stated that our unborn daughter's heartbeat was dropping, and an emergency C-section would need to be performed. Suzi and I gave our consent, and I was prepped for surgery. The doctors and nurses gave information during the surgery, and when they announced that she was born, I anxiously waited for her cry. I knew that if I could hear this beautiful sound it would mean that my daughter had safely made her entrance into the world. However, her cry didn't come. Unbeknownst to anyone, her umbilical cord had become wrapped around her neck several times in utero, so when she was born she was blue and had trouble breathing. Due to the quick responses of the staff, the scare quickly ended, and after what seemed to be an eternity, I finally heard the cry I had been waiting for. The birth of Isabel solidified the belief that I loved being a mother more than I ever imagined possible. I made a vow to give my children not only my heart, but also the thing I had struggled for years to give anyone - my raw and unwavering commitment.

As the years passed, Suzi and I settled into parenthood and the life we were creating for our little family. During these years, I found myself slipping into what I call "the cloud" or "the dark." Meaning, I spent a significant amount of time and energy planning for the future, worrying about things that were out of my control, and overscheduling myself. I tried to be all things to all people and do, or accomplish, everything that was on my list. With these demands of myself came little time for living in the moment, being present with my children, or simply enjoying what life had to offer. After the children were born, Suzi and I decided that I would work evening hours so that I could be regularly available to the children when they weren't in school. Although this meant that the children were always with one of us, it also meant that I frequently had to work during my time with them, ultimately sacrificing precious time living in the moment. Often I felt extremely torn between professional obligations and personal commitments, which left me saying yes to most social engagements, while remaining a full-time mother and part-time employee. The juggling act left me in an endless cycle of multitasking. I physically would be taking care of the children but mentally preparing for work events or meetings.

Approximately three months after Isabel's birth, I decided to pursue my long held dream of becoming a Licensed Clinical Social Worker. I studied relentlessly for the licensure exam, and in

RECONSTRUCTION

February 2007, I received my official certification. Not long after becoming licensed, I joined a private practice. Within a year's time I opened up my own private practice and began working several nights a week so that I could be both a full-time mother during the day and full-time therapist at night. My drive to grow a successful business and continue to help others, while remaining the perfect mom, actually prevented me from being the best at anything. The truth is, I find it difficult to recall events from this time in my life, because I was always so busy running from one place to the other.

As if I had not taken on enough, I decided it was time to sign up for my first marathon. Unfortunately, I was injured halfway through the training process, and although the doctors recommended that I not continue my training, I was determined to see my dream realized, and forged ahead. Looking back, I realize this was likely a crucial error on my part, as my body was sending me signals that it was reaching a state of overload, but I did not listen. As my training was coming to an end and the day of the marathon was fast approaching, a tiny bump appeared under the skin of my right breast. The small lump was so close to the surface and so close to the outside borders of my breast that it seemed totally innocuous, and I put it out of my mind. I had no indication of what was to come - an even bigger race was right in front of me.

CHAPTER 3
Searching for Answers

Online Health Journal Entry

Riding the Bus
Sep 11, 2013 10:47pm

So do you remember the feeling you had the first time you rode on the big yellow bus? The seats were terribly uncomfortable, it was confusing and noisy, and you felt small and scared as you climbed the dark stairs and headed on to this unknown to ride to who knows where. I watched Juliet get on the bus for the first time this morning and as she sat down in her seat towards the back of the bus and flashed me that all too familiar nervous smile and wave, I realized that this was the perfect metaphor for how I was feeling. Each day I feel like I get on the big yellow bus, and I am uncertain as to where it will take me. I have to put complete trust in a person I do not know, and who might understandably think of me as patient number 367, to get me to the correct destination.

Now do not get me wrong, I have some good moments. Tonight for example, Suzi and I had a wonderful dinner complete with a fabulous glass of wine and a rather large Lobster. We strolled the streets, and I even managed, for about one whole minute, to forget that I was facing this battle. Sadly, though, cancer always manages to creep back in like crab grass does in the heat of the summer. In our feeble attempt to make a joke out of cancer, Suzi and I attempted to think of an appropriate nickname for this unwelcomed guest. We haven't decided on a true winner and welcome any suggestions. We received the unfortunate news that there was at least one cancerous lymph node involved, but the doctors are hopeful that this might be the only one infected. We also received the added bonus of finding out that I am HER 2 borderline. Now I highly recommend that you don't run and look up HER 2 status like I made the mistake of doing. It will not boost your spirits. Apparently if you are deemed positive for this "special" little protein, it means that your cancer is likely more aggressive. The doctors have sent my sample back to the lab for additional testing in order to see if they can sort this out and find a true answer. To be honest, I am beginning to suspect that cancer does not provide anyone with answers...only more questions. It is so fascinating how my expectations have changed since I learned I have cancer. When I first had a biopsy I thought, "Well if my cancer is only in the breast I can handle this." As more information was handed to me, my perspective changed to, "If it was only in one lymph node I can handle this." Now my perspective is "If the cancer has not spread to my other organs, I can handle this." I apologize profusely if the last sentence is hard to read, but truthfully it is so much harder to write and comprehend.

Okay it is time that I turn this pity party around, before you all leave and go to a livelier event. I will end my journal entry with all of the positive things that I have in my life: my family, my friends, my job, and my will. I am so strong willed that I've packed my cancer and myself in the car and we are headed up north to another top rated hospital where we hope to obtain some clarity and a small sense of peace.

Love to All,

M

RECONSTRUCTION

On a hot summer's day in late August, I walked into a busy metropolitan hospital where I would hear the words that no one wants to hear, "YOU HAVE CANCER." To this day, even as I say the words out loud, it is still hard to fully comprehend the complexity and overwhelming nature of what occurred in that moment. As I sat across from a young and kind physician, I instinctively knew the message she would deliver to me. I learned that my life, anyone's life, could be transformed in less than one minute! At the reportedly uncommon young age of thirty-seven, I was told that I had Invasive Ductal Carcinoma, which is generally referred to as Breast Cancer. I distinctly remember the first words I spoke after learning of my diagnosis. Through tearful eyes and an unsteady tone, I turned to the physician and said, "But I have two young small girls. What will I do? WHAT WILL I DO?" I honestly think that for many weeks, I didn't know what to do. Now as I look back, I realize that I always knew deep within myself that if I could somehow hold on, I would come out of this situation a stronger and healthier version of myself. I just didn't know how to get there.

My initial response to my illness was not atypical. I experienced feelings of disbelief, anger, and despair. The first weekend after my diagnosis, a very dear friend, and fellow breast cancer survivor, offered for me to come stay at her family's beach house. I had visited this quaint and peaceful home many times before, but this time was different. At the place that had previously provided comfort, relaxation, and joy, I was lost, afraid, and half alive. I spent several days in a dark room where I alternated between sleeping, panicking, and crying. I was completely grief stricken and emotionally paralyzed. Through those days many thoughts haunted me like: How bad is my cancer? Will I live to see my children grow another year? How do I fight? This would not be the last time I entered into what I now call "the vacuum," but what I would learn in the years to follow was that each time I fought my way out of it, I became stronger and more whole.

Due to the aggressive nature of my breast cancer and lymph node involvement, I was told that I would need six months of chemo and thirty-five treatments of radiation. I approached cancer treatment as I had done everything else in my life: with determination, pure grit, and resilience. However, when facing one's own mortality, even the most stubborn individuals can fall to their knees.

I honestly don't know how I survived the first six months of my diagnosis. It was probably only through the generosity and love provided by so many individuals, some even strangers, and my truly undeniable will to survive that I was able to continue to get up each day and face myself, my family and my uncertain future. i was fortunate enough to have the most amazing support system. I vividly remember the day I walked into my bedroom after returning from the hospital where I had just undergone surgery for a double mastectomy. Sitting in the corner was a beautifully decorated pink Christmas tree, complete with at least thirty presents underneath it. This was truly amazing, as it was in the early weeks of September; however, Christmas had made an early appearance. In the months to follow there would be countless examples of kindness including flowers, cards, and visits. My beautiful sister even took it upon herself to make healthy food for my family and me for months following the diagnosis. She provided us with nurturing meals at a time when I did not even have the strength to cook for my family.

Although I had an amazing support system, an amazing partner, and two beautiful children, there were still days where I felt alone. On several days I felt as though I was standing in a dark room and I could not find my way out. Looking back, I believe the reason I couldn't find my way out was because I had missed the message that the path out of the dark was only found within myself. I learned that I had to completely immerse myself in who I was before cancer, who I was at that moment, and the person I knew I ultimately wanted to become. I believe wholeheartedly that the majority of individuals spend a significant amount of time, fruitlessly attempting to figure out how to please others, to be what they want them to be, and to give them what they expect. I realized that I had to become who I wanted me to be. I had to become someone that I was proud of, someone that I could count on. Only then would others see me in the same light as I saw myself.

My cancer, although diagnosed in the summer of 2013, likely began many years before. Of course I was unaware that a tiny seed was taking hold of a damaged piece of me, and would grow to completely dissolve everything I knew to be true. I first noticed the lump on the bottom left corner of my breast approximately one year earlier. During the changing colors of fall and when training for my first marathon, I initially became aware of this odd and peculiar, but not terribly alarming spot. Based on what I had read the symptoms did not support a typical breast cancer diagnosis, a fact that I would later find common for a handful of survivors. My lump was soft, palpable, extremely close to the surface of my skin, and in the beginning it grew and shrank throughout a month's time. Moreover, I had just had my first mammogram, accompanied by an ultrasound, which I had requested due to the fibrocystic nature of my breasts. The results of the mammogram had been clean which was further confirmation that there was no cause for alarm. And honestly, at that point in my life, cancer was the furthest thing from my mind. I was young, healthy, and had no family history of the illness. In the years to come, I would learn that there were signs, albeit not the typical signs, but I did not slow down long enough to hear my body screaming at me to pay attention. I had discussed the lump with multiple individuals who had agreed that it was likely nothing to worry about. However, after careful consideration, we decided that I should mention it at my next OB/GYN appointment, just to be on the safe side.

During this appointment I casually mentioned the protuberance, and the doctor provided reassurance that she strongly felt that it wasn't anything to be concerned about, but would refer me to a breast cancer specialist. I made the specialist appointment thinking that I was just being overly concerned as usual, but decided to go anyway. The breast cancer specialist I initially saw put my mind at ease, as she explained that this was absolutely not breast cancer and was likely another benign cyst. When I asked her if it needed to be removed, she said that it absolutely did not, but could be if it was bothersome, and that I could take my time in doing so as it was definitely not cancer. What I now know is it that the specialist ignored a critical step in her diagnosis process, which was to biopsy the lump from my breast. Had she done so, we would have known that this was breast cancer six months before the surgery that later removed my cancer, and a full year from when I initially discovered the lump. Based on the information provided at the visit, I asked the physician if I could wait until the end of the summer to have the lump removed, as I had some trips planned and I wanted to be able to get into the water while traveling. Again, she stated this would be perfectly fine and not something to be concerned about since it would be merely a cosmetic surgery. I even went so far as to reach out to the physician's nurse via phone after our appointment to once again confirm the information I had received. I was told again there was no urgency for the surgery. So under the direction of an experienced physician, I decided to wait three months to have the lump removed, a decision that will likely haunt me for the rest of my life.

Several weeks prior to my scheduled surgery date, I requested another appointment, because I was experiencing pain in my right breast - not typically considered a symptom of breast cancer. Several years later, I learned from other survivors that, they too, experienced pain in their breast prior to their official diagnosis. After performing a quick exam and ultrasound, the same doctor I had previously seen explained that change to the size of the lump, if any, was minimal. She advised me to look up the causes of the pain on the Internet and take Primrose Oil. I left the office feeling frustrated and as though I was once again worrying too much, and badgering a physician for information that did not exist. After leaving the office, I immediately called my wife Suzi, told my story, and added that a dear friend had mentioned a women's center within our city that I should explore if I was interested in a second opinion. Immediately Suzi said she thought this was a good idea and that I should just leave the building and call the recommended center for an appointment.

I reached out to the office who was able to schedule me for an appointment for the following Tuesday. It became apparent during this appointment that something *had* changed in my breast, so the doctor immediately performed a mammogram, ultrasound, and an accompanying biopsy. As I neared the end of my visit to the women's center, a beautifully kind physician explained that, although we would need to wait for the pathology results, she believed there was a possibility that I did have breast cancer. She ended the appointment by explaining that she would contact me regarding an additional appointment where we would discuss the biopsy results. I don't know if it was the research I was doing, my intuition, or that I had known all along, but I knew that when I went back to see this doctor she would tell me that I had cancer. Unfortunately, I was right. So, on a sunny day during the summer of 2013, in a small office void of windows (a setting I would later remember as eerily similar to the day we learned of my miscarriage), my journey with cancer would begin.

The first step of my newly identified journey led me to a doctor whom I would ultimately come to hold in extremely high regard. I knew he was the most skilled surgeon for my type of cancer, but my trust in his care would develop slowly because of my past experiences. I had been told by several breast cancer survivors, "Your surgeon is like a one-night stand, you just need them to be great for a brief period of time." So as I went to meet my future one-hit wonder, I did what anyone would do when selecting the best candidate. I armed myself with pages of questions. Truly, I think that I should have been a researcher! After the initial shock and devastation of the diagnosis, I put all of my efforts into learning everything I could about my illness and how best to fight to live. During this time, I learned a great deal about my specific type of cancer, which caused simultaneous feelings of fear and relief.

During my initial meeting with the surgeon, he explained that depending on the results of the scheduled MRI, his recommendation would be to perform a lumpectomy. During surgery, only the tumor and the affected surrounding area would be removed, instead of the entire breast. Following surgery, radiation and medication therapy could be necessary. Despite popular research and practice recommending breast conservation surgery, and thus the above-mentioned lumpectomy, I was adamant from the beginning that I wanted to have a double mastectomy. Both of my breasts would be surgically removed, because I wanted to decrease my fear of the cancer returning. After a few additional conversations related to possible options, the surgeon explained that the decision was ultimately mine, and my double mastectomy was scheduled.

According to the latest information I was reading regarding cancer treatment, a second or even third opinion is often recommended before making a final decision about surgery. So my wife, my breast cancer, and I traveled north to one of the leading cancer hospitals in the world. The center presented much like an extremely well run airport with beautifully appointed decor, well organized staff, and a very long wait. To be truthful, I was hoping to leave the cancer up north with this very capable staff, but in reality, the cancer was mine and mine alone. The staff at the hospital were extremely knowledgeable, caring, and I instantly fell in love with the nurse navigator program; however, after much consideration, I decided that for the sake of my family, and due to a very similar treatment plan provided at the local university, the fate of my life would rest in the hands of the great doctors in Virginia.

If my time with the surgeon was truly a one-night stand, then I would say my night was a huge success. Not only was the cancer skillfully removed, he took thirteen lymph nodes, and I came away with no evidence of cancer remaining in my body, what is called "clean margins." Although this magnificent surgeon might not be the one you would choose to talk to about feelings, he was absolutely the right choice for my treatment, and I feel amazingly grateful that I had him on my team. As much as I would love to say that I sailed through surgery with my pink flag waving, the truth is that the removal of my breasts was both emotionally and physically painful. However, in spite of feelings of inadequacy and deformity, I made the conscious decision to put on my false boobs and reenter the world minus two key parts. The loss of my breasts, and the discovery of my new perspective about my outward appearance, would end the first chapter of my journey into the world of cancer treatment.

* * *

As I first walked into what would later become my daily place of visitation, I was filled with a sense of hope. I felt that somehow the doctor that I was about to meet would wrap me in the arms of oncology and make it all better. The reality of what occurred went something like this: The physician was very knowledgeable, and it was quickly apparent that she had given my case considerable thought; however, I continued to feel overwhelmed by the information provided during the meeting, my emotionally fragile state, and an uncertain future. As I had been told, if the surgeon is your one-night stand, then your oncologist is your lifetime partner. In order to ensure a successful marriage, I again came armed with a list of questions. The most important ones to me were: What did it mean that I had lymph node involvement? What are the chances that I will be here next year? My oncologist reminded me that it was important to take things one-step at a time and to focus on the positives versus the challenges. This was so hard for me, not because I couldn't focus on the positive, but because I needed to know the worst-case scenario so I knew how to fight. During this moment, I thought about the irony that not only had I selected a life partner who was an eternal optimist, but I had also unknowingly chosen this type of individual as my partner in the fight against cancer. Clearly the universe was attempting to teach me something, and as time would reveal, I would learn a great deal about becoming what I've termed a "plantonomist" - someone who attempts to view the world through a positive lens while preparing for moments of uncertainty.

During the initial appointment with the oncologist, she explained that because my cancer had spread from its original site to the nearby lymph nodes, I would require extensive chemotherapy. I was completely on board with this idea, as I had already decided that I wanted to take whatever measures were required in order to survive this ordeal. The doctor also discussed options related to a variety of chemotherapy cocktails, all of which had their own array of possible side effects, but would be essential in significantly increasing my chances of survival.

During this meeting, I also was informed that I had the fortunate opportunity to participate in a clinical trial where I would receive a medication that, according to reported research, is normally reserved for women whose breast cancer is linked with a specific protein. Despite the potential life saving impacts of this medication, there were potentially dangerous side effects including heart damage, which made this an extremely difficult and ironic decision to make. Strangely enough, just one year prior to my diagnosis, my sister had asked me if I ever worried about cancer, and I had quickly said no, as there was not a significant familial link. I told her I was instead concerned about heart disease, as it had been a strong contributor to loss of life within our family. My life had truly come full circle. I had to make the decision as to whether or not I would take a drug that might decrease my chances of a cancer recurrence, but could increase the likelihood of the heart disease I feared the most. Ultimately I decided to accept the invitation to join the trial and was selected as one of the individuals who would receive the medication. I then began to fully immerse myself in what would be the most influential, heart wrenching, and transformative year of my life.

RECONSTRUCTION

As the second leg of my journey came under way, I became acutely aware that I might be labeled as "a difficult patient" as I frequently asked questions, practiced regular self-advocacy, and brought up my body's reactions to treatment to the oncology staff. I actually came to relish this title after reading a book written by the amazing Bernie Siegel, entitled *Love Medicine and Miracles*. In this book I received information that led me to believe that the patients who asked a lot of questions, challenged the medical team when needed, and actively participated in their care, could possibly achieve stronger outcomes. Although I had spent my whole life worrying what other people thought, like whether or not other they liked me and approved of my actions, I finally had courage from this inspiring book. I stopped worrying about pleasing others and started worrying about me and what I needed to prevent my children from losing their mother. This moment was likely the first true step in my reconstruction. Each time I pushed the envelope, asking more questions and facing the doctors head on, I walked away worried about whether or not they approved of my decision or liked me. Then I would tell myself, "But it doesn't matter if they like you. What matters is that your two young children deserve to have their mother, and you will do everything in your power to make this happen." You see, I was, and had to be, my biggest advocate. I had to stand up and be the hero of my own story, because in the end that's all there was - MY STORY.

What did I learn from this time of research, gathering information, and sifting through an enormous amount of unknown material in the hopes to make sense of it all? I believe that the most important thing I gained was that you must be your own advocate. Before cancer I was too mild mannered to question authority, ask the tough questions, and push back when I needed to. When my life depended on it, I found that, not only did I have a voice; I had the innate ability to be heard even at the expense of not being liked. I could no longer sit back and let individuals who were labeled as the experts make key decisions regarding my future and health without my input and approval. I have the utmost respect for each doctor who tirelessly answered my questions and responded to my doubts and fears, but instead of feeling guilty for asking for this level of compassion and care, I came to understand that I, along with every other patient, deserve and am owed this form of response.

Patients are not their illnesses. They are certainly not to be placed in large categories known as breast, prostate, lung, or another form of cancer. Those who bravely fight each and every day to take back their lives reserve the right to ask ten different questions, in ten different ways, and to ask them as many times as needed. They must be given space to do this in order to feel comforted during an otherwise chaotic time. Furthermore, a patient should not be considered difficult simply because he or she is a highly active participant in their own care, nor should they be dismissed as an overly anxious individual simply because they report on a multitude of symptoms. I became the expert in my illness, and therefore, in my care. The physicians played crucial and undeniable roles vital to my survival, but when everyone else went home at night, leaving cancer at the office, I was left with my illness. I needed to be my biggest advocate, the champion of my own survival.

RECONSTRUCTION

CHAPTER 4
Surviving the Red Devil

Online Health Journal Entry

My First Weekend with the Red Devil
Oct 20, 2013 8:58pm

When you go on match.com, do not and I repeat do not start chatting with, winking at, or private messaging any mysterious member called the Red Devil. This she-devil will chew you up and spit you out, and then she will leave you holding the bill. I will not go into all of the details of my weekend with the Red Devil, as they are boring and a bit traumatic, but what I would like to talk about are the great things that happened during my weekend.

First: I successfully attended a great work event (without getting sick on anyone. YAY!) By the way, I truly have the best boss in the world. Second: My sister made me the most fabulous mashed potatoes, which might have saved my life, and we received a surprise visit from Kirsten and Tracey on Friday. Third: I never thought I would weep when Katie asked me if I wanted a bean burrito (the only thing I could eat when I was pregnant.) Fourth: I received two beautiful floral arrangements on Friday. Fifth: My in-laws took my daughters on Saturday, which was so good for them. Sixth: I received the most wonderful text messages and calls.

Seventh: Most importantly, Suzi never left my side, which was the most comforting and wonderful gift I could have received. As a bonus: I was able to read two books to Izzy before she went to bed this evening which made me feel like a mom again.

So with all of the bad that there was, there were so many wonderful things that occurred during my first weekend with the Red Devil.

By the way, please excuse any current or future grammatical errors as it is due to the medicine. That is my story and I am sticking to it!

Love to All,

M

Chemotherapy was a lesson in the raw undeniable will to survive, and it forced me to slow down. My cancer treatment was divided into two sections. The first was a medication Adriamycin, commonly referred to as the "Red Devil" (due to it's deep red color and ravaging effects on the body.) Let me tell you, it wholeheartedly lives up to its name. In addition to the intense treatments, I also received an injection of an immune boosting medication. I spent the first three days following each infusion of the Red Devil desperately trying to maintain some semblance of normalcy. The next seven to ten days were lost to a dark bedroom and bathroom, where constant sickness and feelings of isolation were common. Initially, I thought maybe I had been slightly mislead regarding the side effects of the medicine, as for the first couple of days following an infusion, I continued to participate in life, and could even take in small amounts of food. But after I received an injection of an immune boosting medication, I was transported to a whole new level of suffering. These were the times when the hero would have to take over. They were times of tears, doubt, and also a complete raw desire for life.

There were many days when I didn't think I could keep allowing a medication into my body that was hopefully eradicating cancer cells, while simultaneously destroying my physical and emotional being. The anticipation of the immense suffering would initiate a deep sense of anxiety, but then out of nowhere the hero would rise, and I would once again return to battle the Red Devil. During these treatments, I spent time visiting with Suzi, updating my personal online health journal, or taking much needed naps. I actually have fond memories of the hours at the chemotherapy facility, as the nurses were so kind, and it forced me to slow down and focus on the most essential components of life: laughter, love, rest, food, and living. This was an important lesson that I was learning, as I had never before taken time for myself. Prior to the diagnosis, I had established a successful business and raced through life attempting to balance work and family, leaving little to no time for self-care. After receiving my diagnosis, I closed my therapy practice, as I could not ask my patients to wait for my return. It was terribly sad but I knew it was the right thing to do. This was the journey that I needed to be on. As a social worker, mother, and wife I had spent a significant amount of time taking care of others, but with cancer I was forced to take time to take care of myself first, and become more open to accepting help from others.

As if cancer treatment and managing a new normal was not a large enough journey, my family, true to form, was simultaneously traveling down another path full of adventure and excitement. Roughly six months prior to my cancer diagnosis, our family had decided that Suzi would work toward fulfilling her lifelong dream of becoming an Ironman. This was a huge endeavor. An Ironman race is one in which an individual swims 2.4 miles, bikes 112 miles, and completes a marathon, all in the allotted fifteen-hour time limit. Did I mention that my wife never does anything halfway? Well, not only did we decide that she would work toward meeting this goal, we also elected to have her join a training team that raised money for Multiple Myeloma cancer research. Keep in mind that we signed up for this training team nearly six months prior to the cancer diagnosis, so I find it ironic that on the day I came home from my double mastectomy surgery, my wife Suzi hosted a fundraising event for Multiple Myeloma - she would ultimately raise $30,000 for the organization. As part of the fundraising mission, Suzi had signed up for the Florida Ironman, which happened to take place at the same time that I was in the depths of treatment. Although we debated whether or not she should still participate, in the end I stated that it was important to me that she kept going...that she run when I could not walk, swim when I was drowning, and bike when the wheels had just fallen off of mine.

When Suzi first signed up for the race we decided that it would be a family affair, and that the girls and I would be there to cheer her on, but as treatment progressed, it became increasingly clear that this would be impossible. It is amazing how much strength you can gain from steroids! One evening, in my steroid fog, I decided I would surprise Suzi by getting on a train and traveling twenty-four hours to Florida, where I would be waiting at the finish line. We always supported one another in all of our sporting events, and I could not imagine not being there for this one. I honestly believe that the thought of not attending this event was harder for me than the chemotherapy medications traveling through by body.

As the time drew closer, my mother realized how serious I was about getting on the train. Unbeknownst to me, she devised a plan to somehow knock me out, so I couldn't get on the train and actually go through with my idea. Lucky for her, I eventually came to the sad realization that as much as I longed to be at the race, it was more important that I remain behind. Thankfully there are people in your life that are more than friends - they are the glue that holds you together in times of struggle. Just as the sticky substance surrounds what's broken to create a strong and unbreakable bond, so did my friends the night of Suzi's race. My eight-mama army, as we had come to call one another, arrived at my house on that amazing evening, where we watched Suzi's lifelong dream come to life on a small computer screen. Honestly, due to the effects of steroids and pain medication, I don't remember the whole night, but I do remember Suzi crossing the finish line. Tears rolled down my face, happiness mixed with deep sadness - happy for her accomplishment and sad that I wasn't able to be there. As it happened many times during my journey, this was a time of learning, as before cancer I would've been on that train; I would have forced myself beyond my limits, but this time I could not, and no amount of stubbornness was going to help me make that train. So with much protest and dissatisfaction, I learned that sometimes we have to first put on our oxygen mask before we can ever successfully help someone else.

* * *

About halfway through my dance with the Red Devil, I noticed that my hair was beginning to thin, and decided it was time to shave my head. I had decided early on that I would be the one to take my hair and not the illness I was fighting. Amazingly enough, this was not a fearful event, as I had witnessed a friend participate in the head shaving ritual, and hair was not really that important to me, or at least I didn't think it was at the time. Once again, my army of eight mamas gathered together, and not only did I shave my head that night, but several others joined in on the fun, including my beautiful wife, who sported a military cut complete with a blonde dye job for many months to come. Sometime after that night I fully grasped the level of solidarity that was present in the room. We did not mourn the loss of my hair, but celebrated my ability to take control of my life, and it strengthened the bond of eight beautiful women.

Once it became apparent that my GI Jane haircut would soon be replaced with a bowling ball appearance, I made the decision that it was time to go wig shopping. Much like breast prosthesis shopping it was not glamorous or uplifting, but rather, a reminder that I was slowly losing pieces of my outward identity. I entered a small room with no windows in a busy hospital setting where I found a kind woman, who took more than an hour to assist me with picking out a wig, that I have to tell you, I never wore. I gave the wig an honest try, but it just was not for me, as it seemed to shine a light on my illness. Since it was in the winter months when I lost my hair, I decided that I would, instead, wear beautifully knitted caps. Lucky for me, there are magic volunteers that knit caps for individuals who have lost their hair. When I entered the treatment facility every three weeks, I was fortunate enough to go shopping for another lovingly created gift. Anyone who has lost his or her hair can attest to the fact that the winter is the worst time to lose your hair. When you are sleeping, the cold can be felt from your scalp down. I began to need to sleep under the covers with a cap on my head. Somehow, these caps made me feel safe and protected, and to this day I will often don some of the same caps during the winter months. The caps came to be yet another connection to others. Amazingly, I was receiving love and support from individuals that I had never even met. Without even noticing, I was slowly learning the depth at which we as humans are interconnected, and that the ripple effect of kindness is ongoing - after my hair grew back I donated most of my caps to help others.

It's interesting how we can begin to associate certain things with life experiences. For example, although I instinctively knew that three days following the infusions I would experience significant suffering, I strangely began to find positive aspects of my time spent at the facility. By the middle of my treatment regimen, I had somewhat of a schedule, where either my wife or one of my dear friends or family member would drive me to the facility. Once there, we would settle into one of the rooms, and as the steroid began to enter my system, I would become instantly hungry. My amazing companion would go and pick up my favorite Panera treat.

Since the physicians knew early on that I would need chemotherapy, a port was placed in the left of my chest that was used to transport the medication throughout my body. With this port in place, the medications are set up so that you can still walk around while rolling a poll that holds the bags of medicine. Anyone who knows me knows that I love to talk to others and ensure that they are doing okay, so as the medication flowed through my body, I would, unsteadily (due to the anti nausea drugs), pull my little pole of medication and visit with the other patients. Looking back, I guess the lunch, the visitors, and the interactions with other cancer patients, were my attempts to normalize an otherwise scary and uncertain situation. When I was asking others how they were doing or I was spending the time with those that I love, I felt that I was in some way still connected to the world around me. So in a strange way, walking around with a pole of medications following behind me, rather than just sitting and waiting, was symbolic of not letting cancer keep me from living my life.

My relationship with the Red Devil came to an end on December 2, 2013. I was not sad to end this torrid affair, however, as with any unhealthy relationship, I learned many lessons and it would continue to fuel a change within me. I believe that the most crucial piece of this battle, the thing that I would come to lean on in times of great despair and hopelessness, was that I had survived cancer treatments. Not only did I make it through, but also the very fiber of my being was both strengthened and reaffirmed with each fighting moment. My resolve to live and truly embrace everything that life had to offer was intensified, and a clearer focus about my ultimate purpose was established. I think when you're too sick to focus on anything but basic human needs like eating, sleeping, human touch, and simply surviving, all of the other noise fades away, and you see it is just you and the life before you.

* * *

Online Health Journal

Two Down
Nov 5, 2013 5:31pm

I was brought to my knees, and when I looked up, there you were. I will never be able to thank you enough for everything you have done for my family and me. Just when I thought there was not a thing left to give, you bring more flowers, send more cards, deliver loving messages, and so much more. I can honestly say that I have never had to fight so hard to make it just one more day and at the exact same time, I have never felt so loved, supported, and protected in my whole life. Please forgive me but I have fallen behind on thank you notes as the generosity overwhelms me emotionally and makes it quite challenging to maintain my southern manners. For those of you who are reading this message let me just say I love you and I love hearing from you, even if I find it hard to respond. I try very hard to respond to each email and text but I must admit the chemotherapy has been much more difficult than I initially anticipated, and it normally takes me about 4-5 days to recover. I have conquered the Red Devil twice with two battles remaining. I will then receive twelve rounds of Taxol, which I have been told is an easier medication. Although this journey has been so very difficult I am learning so many things about my relationships, my spirituality, my strength, and myself. I have been rocked to my very core and there are moments when I do not know how I will go on, but go on I do! One amazing thing that has happened is that I have joined a fantastic organization called Beyond Boobs. This wonderful support group provides guidance, comfort, and love to young women diagnosed with breast cancer. On a final note I want to take a moment and recognize all of your amazing accomplishments.

Love to All,

M

* * *

How do we survive times of great trial and tribulation? I believe the answer is both complicated and simple. It was amazingly easy to get up each day and face the daily battle in front of me when the thing that I was fighting for was clear and undeniable. After becoming a parent for the first time, I experienced a significant understanding of what it means to love someone more than myself. The deep love I felt by giving my heart to this small and amazing human being brought both a greater sense of purpose, and a determination to be a better person. I drew on this strong bond with my children during my illness, and would literally say to myself, "I will get up today, if not for me, then for my children." Moreover, I was determined in my resolve to do everything in my power to remain with my children so that they didn't experience the loss of a parent at a young age, as I had. I want to make it clear that I am not saying that I would have failed my children had I not been able to physically overcome my illness. Rather, I am describing a time when my love for my children became a beacon of hope, strength, and inspiration.

While surviving physically was something that fueled my parental instincts, my need to remain emotionally present during this battle meant a complete breakdown of the person I once knew, and a necessary overhaul of myself. My emotional sense of self before cancer was built on a fragile frame, one that required constant rebuilding and protection from the external elements. I had spent most of my life fearing rejection and abandonment, which ultimately led to desperate measures to achieve belonging and self-worth. Instead of focusing on the development of my inner identity, I spent the majority of my life pouring attention and focus into living up to the expectations of others, and searching for external acceptance and love. Due my life experiences and a predominant lack of self-worth, I entered into cancer treatment feeling lost, insecure, and uncertain. Since my emotional foundation was initially built with materials unable to weather a storm, it could easily come crashing down. At that time, I did not realize that the ultimate collapse of the person I had come to know as myself was the beginning of the individual that I would eventually come to love.

In the face of great trauma, the process of hitting rock bottom can be swift and impactful, or it can be slow and unpredictable. Sometimes this all-encompassing losing of one's self is a combination of many moments in time. I did not know, nor did I recognize, that the bottom was slowly but undeniably dropping out from under my feet. In light of the overwhelming physical and emotional toll of cancer treatments, I believed that I was adequately coping with my illness. The truth was that I was drowning in a sea of uncertainty, fear, and grief, and no matter how fast or hard I swam, I could not reach the shore.

There were evolving signs during my journey that I was beginning to slip deeper within, and losing a grasp on those that I loved and the external world that once held so much promise and possibility to me. I remember moments when I did not get out of bed, not just because I was physically spent, but also because I was emotionally barren. I found myself repeating the words "I have nothing left to give." There were times when the enormity of grief, loss, and fear was more than I could emotionally carry, and so I would fall to my knees, not knowing how to stand and face my unstable reality once again. When I first began chemotherapy, I was determined to physically contribute to the world around me, and would attempt to continue my regular activities like weekend running and full-time work. As treatment continued and the physical challenges of it became more apparent, my emotional capacity to exert energy, and a high level of commitment to those things I once cherished, became increasingly diminished. To be blunt, although I was determined to physically remain present for the family I loved, I was losing the will to emotionally connect to the life I once lived and the individuals I held so dear.

I do think that my experience, albeit painful and paralyzing, was also a normal response to a significant loss, and that this downward decline was necessary in order for me to find the truth and my own sense of power and strength. I had to witness the internal collapse of my self in order to connect with my basic core and personally claim my individuality and empowerment. Hitting rock bottom was not just an inevitable process. It was crucial to my overall reconstruction, as it provided the ability to reprioritize life and those persons, things, and moments that I spent time and energy on. I learned through illness about health, and through suffering I gained a deeper appreciation for recovery. After a much needed break from chemotherapy, and one amazing family holiday where spending time together replaced seasonal shopping, and gratitude for life and health replaced the stress of perfectly wrapped presents, I entered into the second phase of chemotherapy treatment. Here, the words "will to survive," would take on a much deeper meaning, and the discovery of myself would ultimately occur.

In the end, what do we learn from the battles we have won and those we have gracefully lost? I think that this question is better answered by asking: Having survived this struggle, how can I learn to thrive in the midst of great adversity? I believe that survival correlates with our basic instinct for continued existence, and that it has historically been linked to the notion that in order to survive, one must possess a certain level of physical strength and stamina. I pose the following question: How often do you equate the act of surviving with impactful and sustaining change and reconstruction? After a population survives a flood, we often discuss how they have rebuilt their homes and cities, but when do we talk about how we will build structures differently in order to better withstand the inevitable future storms? I think we can't simply discuss how we made it through; we must instead open our hearts and minds to *why* we made through and what we have learned. Since I am neither a scientist, nor a physician, I will not profess to know for certain what constitutes true survival. However, as a social worker and someone who has battled cancer and has come out on the other side, I will say that I physically withstood the effects and treatments of my trauma, but more importantly I grew both emotionally and physically from the experience. This is exactly where the concept of thriving comes into play. For me, it was not enough to physically exist following this long battle. It was essential that I evolved as a human being. I wish I could replicate my raw and unwavering desire to be transformed so that I could share it with others, because it is a feeling that I would carry with me from that moment on, and life as I knew it would never be the same.

RECONSTRUCTION

CHAPTER 5
Rock Bottom

Online Health Journal Entry

Breakfast at Tiffany's
Feb 2, 2014 10:40am

So I finally watched the movie Breakfast at Tiffany's and I must say, although I was not sure what to expect, I must admit that it did not inspire me in the way that I thought that it would. Not that it was not a good movie because it was a beautiful reminder of the simplicities of another time; however, I guess I was just expecting to fall in love instantly with the plot and characters, which I unfortunately did not. This introduction leads me to the point of this long overdue entry, which is; expectations can be foolish and at times even dangerous. I mistakenly thought that receiving this cancer diagnosis would be an opportunity to view life through a new and improved lens and would strengthen me in so many ways, and although it has done those things, it has unfortunately come with a sad price. I have the unfortunate honor to officially have a stalker. This is what my amazing support group, Beyond Boobs, labels the fear that creeps in regarding reoccurrence. The funny thing about a stalker is that they are not someone you can battle face to face, because they are sneaky and show up when you least expect them. In addition, they have the ability to place a cloud over the most beautiful day or moment. In the beginning of my diagnosis I would blame myself if the stalker paid a visit, feeling as if I was not confident enough in my recovery or survival. I have since realized that this feeling is a part of the journey, and as scary as the stalker is, having this mystery shadow also helps me to appreciate my family at a deeper level, listen to my friends more closely, and take time to sit in my favorite chair to read a book. You see the stalker is both a blessing and a curse, never letting me forget that life is short and that sometimes you just have to get out of bed and spend breakfast at Tiffany's.

On a different note, I have 6 more rounds of what will be a total of 16 rounds of chemotherapy. I will then have 7 weeks of radiation, 5 days per week. I have decided to think of my radiation as a time of lying in the sun in Mexico or The Dominican Republic, with Suzi by my side. All I really need now is to line up someone to bring drinks to my beach chair. Following the radiation, I will continue to receive an immunotherapy chemotherapy drug once every three weeks until next December. Now, with all of this treatment one might say my cancer is pretty serious and to be honest they would be accurate, but let's face it, what cancer is not serious. Often times cancer types are compared to one another, stages are discussed, and lymph node status is either celebrated or feared. Well the truth is no matter the type; stage, or status, cancer is life changing and can be both scary and motivating all at the same time. Cancer has made me strive to love Suzi more deeply, love my children more freely, love my friends and family more honestly, and love myself more wholly. Thank you for reading this post and continuing to be an inspiration.

Love to All,

M

RECONSTRUCTION

The second round of chemotherapy came with great changes, both physically and emotionally. As fall turned into winter and the first snow fell, so did my tenacious spirit. I had the distinct feeling that I was losing pieces of myself at an increased speed. With this came great hopelessness. There were days when I could not get out of bed because either I was too weak, my heart was too heavy, or because fear would rap its chains around me and not let go. During this time, I began to discover the essential secret that would begin a complete restructuring of my life.

I did not recognize myself after I lost my eyebrows. When I looked in the mirror, I rationally knew that I saw the same familiar face, but I could no longer connect this broken woman to the person I once was. Combined with continuous physical symptoms such body aches, chills, and an undeniable level of debilitation, I began a descent into a lonely abyss. While the chills would leave me utterly paralyzed and running for the safety of my bed, the body aches would literally and figuratively knock me flat on my back. The metaphor of "hiding under the covers" was perfect for this time in my life, and it eerily reminded me of sheltering myself from childhood fears and insecurities. I have a vivid memory of when I was little and would sleep with my head under the covers in order to escape the monsters lurking in the night. In my childhood reality, I felt that if laid perfectly still and remained silent, I would be safe. Thirty years later, I was seeking comfort, warmth, and safety under the covers once again, as if I could create a shelter for my weary self. As if the side effects of cancer were not enough to make me run for cover, tremendous feelings of guilt and self-loathing, that came from unintentionally abandoning my family for hours or even days, were likely the most unbearable part of the traumatic event. The true seriousness of my condition struck when I least expected it, and I was completely unprepared. On a cold December morning, my family was preparing for my daughter's fifth birthday party. With great sadness and protest from the mother within me, we decided that I was too ill to attend this special occasion. In that fragile moment, I felt the last morsel of connection to my life slip from my grasp. For a season following that day, I would secretly have terrifying, yet eerily calm visions, of a world without me in it. I would ask questions of myself like, "Will Suzi remember to tell them I love them?" and "Will she think to pack their rain coats when it looks like rain?" The darkness experienced during cancer treatment can pull you in and slowly take your soul. When this black cloud begins to whisper your name, you must cling to anything and everything in order to find the way out, even if it is through a different door than you used to get there. Just when I thought I could no longer hold on, I realized that if I didn't reconnect to those I loved and the world around me, then all of the chemo, pain, and suffering would be for nothing. So with a face I no longer recognized and a body that I felt had betrayed me, I got up, showered off, and once again chose to take part in the only life I had.

Anyone who knows me knows that before cancer, and to some extent even after this trauma, I am a self-professed worrier, constantly second-guessing my health, my relationships, and even my own mind. Interestingly, receiving my cancer diagnosis permanently changed my perspective. Instead of worrying about clean hands and waiting emails, I began focusing on being around to see my children grow. I began to realize that my life was a much more legitimate thing to worry about than what others thought of me. Also, I learned that there are times when I just have to let go and live!

Once I began the next chemotherapy regimen, I traded nausea for debilitating aches and pains, and steroid side effects for extreme fatigue. The short and extreme side effects I had grown accustomed to were replaced by long and torturous ones. As hard as the second round of chemotherapy was, I was determined to finish my treatment and found moments of happiness and gratitude in simple things like the beautiful faces of my daughters. When my children looked into my eyes, they did not see a broken and battered person. Rather, they saw the mother they had always loved.

I vividly remember the end of one of my treatments, when the clinical trials nurse came into my room and told me that my neutrophil count was down. She explained that if it dropped to a certain point, which it was close to doing, I would not be able to finish my prescribed chemotherapy treatment. After hearing this, I asked the nurse what I could do to help increase this number. She told me this wasn't something I could personally control, and that we would just have to wait and see if the count would continue to decrease. I am now convinced that this nurse wasn't aware of who she was talking to. To me, hearing her say that was like a double dare, and I was determined to succeed. When I left the treatment facility, I went directly home and did all the research I could on how to increase my immune system's response to the effects of chemotherapy, and found a couple of possible natural methods. After organizing the potential options, I knew instantly who I needed to recruit for this very special mission - my wonderful sister. She immediately got to work creating food that was nutritionally beneficial and that also reportedly assisted with physical healing and wellness. I honestly don't have any scientific evidence that the steps I took changed the direction in which my body was heading, but when I went back to the center for my next round of treatment, my numbers were not just better, but significantly better. The staff instructed me to keep doing whatever I was doing, and so I did. This was the beginning of a significant change in my food choices, and one that I considered to be not just a temporary diet, but a new way in which to live.

One year before my diagnosis, my wife gave me the name "Too Stubborn to Fail" when I was training for what would be my first, and last, marathon. Halfway through my training, I had experienced a significant knee injury that normally would have meant the end of my marathon training and a long time dream, but not for this determined young woman. The sports physician I initially met with told me that I would likely not be able to complete the training, nor the race, which (of course) ignited in me a sheer will to overcome the hurdle. In true Melissa fashion, I quickly set to work, finding possible ways in which to successfully complete the race. Through my research, I discovered I could train by water running, which I must describe here, if only for the sheer humor. Imagine all five foot two inches of me, with a large orange flotation device strapped around my waist, while running in a pool with ten other women, all of retirement age. The truth is, I did not mind this time, as I had the opportunity to meet some wonderful individuals, and I learned an invaluable lesson that would serve me well over the next three years and beyond. I realized that in the face of great adversity, I was stronger and more determined than I thought. Fast forward a year and a half later, and I was sitting in a cancer treatment room, again surrounded by people twice my age. Just like before, I did not mind, as it was a reminder that despite human differences and the individual battles we fight, we continuously remain connected.

Toward the end of my treatment, after I had completed my second round of chemotherapy, I met a physician who taught me the true meaning of empathy. Unbeknownst to him, his tireless work with me helped to heal the significant level of distrust and deep wounds I had from my initial misdiagnosis and dismissal of symptoms. As I sat in the small, but intimidating radiation office, a very tall, and soft-spoken physician walked in, and during the course of one hour, helped me to feel somewhat whole again. To my hospital's credit, all of my doctors were both knowledgeable and hard working, and often times had overflowing caseloads of individuals with desperate needs. But this man completely blew me away with his amazing capacity for compassionate treatment and his ability put my mind at ease. To this day, I tear up when I think of the care provided by this completely selfless doctor, and I feel so thankful to have had him in my corner. As usual, I came to our meeting armed with a multitude of questions, which he patiently and easily answered. In fact, he demonstrated a sense of solidarity with regard to my treatment plan. Furthermore, as I explained to him that I wanted to be aggressive with the radiation, he steadfastly agreed that this was the appropriate course of action, which provided me the validation I had been searching for.

Radiation was a lot easier than chemo in many ways, but it was also very isolating. The treatment was administered each day, with the exception of Saturday and Sunday, and lasted for thirty-five days. It required me to lie on a metal table with my bare chest exposed. During treatments, I was instructed not to move due to the precise nature of the radiation field. As I lay on the cold table, a multitude of thoughts and feelings would come rushing in, and since I could not move, the tears would just come, flow freely, and remain. Radiation taught me a lesson in visualization and how to sit calmly with the things that were deep within me. Since there was no one to talk to and nothing to distract me from fears and unanswered questions, it was essential that I learn to become my own best friend, a task that had evaded me during my previous thirty-six years.

I felt extremely fortunate that during ongoing cancer treatment, I was able to participate in a clinical trial to receive the medication Herceptin. I began receiving this specialized form of immunotherapy after the start of my second round of regular chemotherapy. At the beginning, I was given the medication on a weekly basis; however, once I finished the accompanying chemotherapy medication, a more concentrated dose of Herceptin was provided every three weeks. Soon after this change in my clinical trial medication, I began experiencing increasingly intense and frequent heart palpitations. My doctors decided that one of my infusions should take place in the hospital where they could monitor my body's response to the medicine. After much discussion and exploration, the doctors and nurses discovered that I appeared to be experiencing supraventricular tachycardia, and the clinical trial medication was unfortunately discontinued. I experienced mixed emotions related to this termination, as I firmly believed that this medicine would help prevent reoccurrence, but if my heart could not withstand the treatment then it would not matter if the cancer returned. Looking back, I know that I made the right decision. Just recently, I was speaking to my heart doctor who explained that he ultimately felt that I had experienced mild cardiomyopathy, which, if left untreated, can lead to serious complications. After years of treatment, I have realized that sometimes we have to just listen to our bodies and allow them to point us in the right direction.

What exactly does it feel like when the bottom drops out? From my experience, I was left with the feeling of being lost in a barren field, down an isolated winding road, with no real connections to the world I once knew. I distinctly remember times when I felt half alive and would walk around in a state of what I call, "the invisible presence." Although I was physically present and going through the motions of my life, I found it increasingly hard to be emotionally available. I had the feeling that it was hard for others to know exactly how to connect with me as well. For me, cancer was what I imagined it would feel like to be lost at sea with no land in sight on which to find my footing and claim the right to live. Each new treatment and discussion of my prognosis was like a wave crashing down on me, with moments when I could not stand up and catch my breath. In the darkest of my hours, I felt myself sinking, despite my great efforts to stay afloat, and I mostly feared that I would drown.

Rounds of steroids, pain medications, and hours spent in the bed began to cloud my memory and thoughts. The little energy I had went to spending time with those closest to me, a concept that also would become ingrained in my mind. As my health faded, and at the urging of my amazing radiation doctor, I reluctantly began to accept the fact that I needed to go on short-term disability at work. Once I finally conceded to the idea that I would not be returning to work for at least twelve weeks, my world began to open up in an unexpected way. Since my disability coincided with my daughters' summer break, our family took the opportunity and planned a trip to see a dear friend of twenty years who had moved to Michigan several years prior. Suzi and I decided that since the drive needed to be broken into two days, we would seize the moment and create great adventures along the way for the children. The trip was simply amazing - filled with laughter, sightseeing, lots of love, and was yet another example of how letting go of what is *planned*, and embracing what *is*, can allow for amazing moments to arise. During the trip, I did experience times of fear, desperation, and panic, but instead of allowing these moments to consume me, I made the conscious choice to connect with life around me, if only for a moment, in the hopes that I would not again disappear. During this time in my cancer journey, I learned what resiliency truly was, and that despite all of the treatments and great loss I had been through, I could maintain and even create a new and stronger version of the woman lost in the mirror.

I proudly completed radiation treatment in July 2014, and began taking a daily maintenance medication that would hopefully prevent the reoccurrence of my hormone driven breast cancer. In the fall of that same year, I elected to have a surgery to remove my ovaries in the hopes that this would further decrease the estrogen production within my body, and therefore increase my overall chances of survival. With the exception of medication management, I hoped the surgery would be the last step on my path with Western medicine treatment. It was just the beginning of my relationship with alternative therapies.

It's said that anyone who fights cancer is brave and strong, and I don't disagree with that statement. But as anyone who has battled this illness will tell you, it is after the treatment ends that the real work begins. The thing that understandably escapes most individuals is that when the doctors move their focus to patients with more pressing needs than your own, the meals stop coming, and the silence returns. This is when the fear and doubt wage their private war against the cancer survivor. Someone once said, "I know that you wish you could take a break from cancer." My thought was that cancer is a part of me now, and for me, taking a break is not really in the cards. I do not mean that I am ultimately defined by this experience; however, it's an undeniable part of my existence. I have chosen to heal and strengthen my body from within instead of fighting what some consider to be a foreign entity invading the body.

Prior to chemotherapy, Suzi gave me a pair of cowgirl boots that were made the year I was born. I wore these boots to each and every treatment, and referred to them as my "kicking cancer's ass boots." My beautifully rugged footwear became a symbol of strength and determination, and now when I am wearing the boots, I feel powerful and grounded. I compare the symbolic feeling of wearing the boots to getting up and continuing to live, even when it is so very hard and overwhelming. What I have learned over the years is that, as much as I want to, I cannot escape this cancer diagnosis. I cannot run away, and I cannot hide. What I am left with, however, is the ability to find a way to thrive, and the ability to uncover my new path. There are times when this is so much harder than it appears to be, and moments when I feel trapped in my own reality.

One example happened shortly after visiting the local gym, following a cancer treatment. Since I was raised in a house with two sisters, I had experienced little modesty in the locker rooms and never considered changing behind a curtain; however, this day at the gym would be different. In the blink of an eye, I would see the world through a completely different lens. I walked into the locker room, just as I had a hundred times before, but as I placed my bag on the bench and reached up to take off my shirt; I paused in horror as I realized what was about to happen. If I took off my shirt, it would reveal a woman with scars where breasts used to be, a womanly figure replaced by a sunken chest. I stood there for what felt like forever, panicked as to what I should do next, and then I spotted a small changing room off to the side that gratefully had a curtain. So with tears forming in my eyes I, for the first time in my life, took cover behind the curtain. I am completely aware that, in truth, this was a small price to pay for being alive, but the realization of my physical deformity and difference was both shattering and painful. These feelings of separation from the world around me made it even more important to focus on the simple fact that, despite physical changes and limitations, I could continue to live a full life, and that any physical challenge has the overwhelming capacity to create an amazing sense of internal strength.

When the pieces have come crashing down, and the parts of our once normal life have fallen to the ground, what is the next move, and how in the world do we begin to pick ourselves up and put things back together? If I were to exert every ounce of concentration I possess, I might be able to conjure up the smallest memory of my life before cancer. Don't get me wrong, I still remember the birth of my children, my wedding day, and a handful of other moments, but on a whole, the connection I held to my pre-cancer life is fading. I am truly at peace with this separation. I am sure you are asking, "Why would I be so okay with letting go of the life I had before?" and the answer is simple, as I see it. For the first time in my life, I am learning how to live in the moment. It doesn't mean that I don't take with me the lessons I have learned in the past or my history's beautiful components. It simply means that I have stopped being the person behind the camera and have started being the one in the picture.

The concept of time is a funny thing. We hurry to get to work, school, to the next place in our life, but where do we truly end up? From what I know, most human beings, especially when young, roam the earth with a sense of innocence as it relates to time spent and time that remains. That feeling is something I will never have again, as I am all too aware of possible time remaining, and I often feel as though I can feel the clock ticking faster and faster. I might not experience the great freedom that naivety and ignorance provide, but I have a secret. *I have the ability to realize what is most important, and the knowledge that to take things for granted is equivalent to ignoring my life's purpose and true identity.* Sometimes I feel like I am walking down a path with overgrown trees, and although I can't make out the exact path, I know I must go on, and have faith that I'm headed in the right direction. I guess the ultimate lesson is that, on this walk of life, we are almost guaranteed rough and uncertain terrain, so make sure you pack your big girl boots!

CHAPTER 6
Standing in the Sun

Online Health Journal Entry

Nobody promised you a rose garden
Mar 8, 2014 10:43am

Let me start my post with a grateful thought for the day. Today I am most grateful that it is not snowing, that my children finally feel better, for Suzi, and that I am alive.

The reality of life is that we have good days and we have bad days. To force one's self into pretending that every day is going to be filled with sunshine, roses (which I am not sure why this is since they have thorns), and lightness would be to ignore the fact that with the sweet must come the sour. The truth is that in order to truly appreciate the sweet parts of life, we must endure the sour moments. I appreciate more now than ever the moments when I feel physically, emotionally, and spiritually strong. I wish that I could say today was one of those days, but sadly it is not. Mainly the steroids are to blame as they make me feel like I am on top of the world for about 24 hours, and then they send me crashing to the ground with tears that never end and a heavy cloud that seems to hang endlessly over my head. The good news is that with the sour comes the sweet, and within 48 hours the steroids are gone. I have one more treatment to go and with this will come a mix of emotions. I am so very happy to be closing this chapter of my life, but ironically I will miss the nurses at Stony Point. They have been so amazing. I will also miss talking with the other patients and being there to answer questions for those who are just beginning their journey. When I would enter the treatment room and take snacks to the staff or reassure someone that they would make it through their surgery, I felt good about making someone else's day a little easier. Although I will still be going back every 3 weeks, it somehow feels like it will be different. When I did these things I felt as though, even for a moment, that I was not a cancer patient but a person. The human face of illness, whatever the illness, takes the power from the "thing" and gives the "thing" a name, a face, and a person who other people can relate to. At the treatment center I am not known as the woman with breast cancer. I am known as the woman with the fantastic boots (thanks to Suzi), and the patient who brings snacks. I guess I am afraid to not be that person anymore because that person felt strong and empowered.

So now the update. One more intensive chemo left, 7 weeks of radiation, and every 3 weeks the less intensive chemotherapy drug Herceptin until next December. I would be lying if I said that I am not tired or drained, because I am. But I am here and for that I am so very grateful and feel so amazingly blessed. Because the truth is that I was never promised a rose garden, which is fine by me, because I have always preferred tulips. Here is to spring and the new life it brings.

Love to All,

M

Cancer undeniably takes a toll, not only a person's body, but also wreaks havoc on the deepest parts on one's soul. The illness does, however, also provide certain gifts such as perspective, reasons to fight, a larger capacity for love, and the ability to forgive. At the end of treatment, I must admit, I felt beaten, and at times did not know how to start rebuilding. Honestly, reconstruction, at the time, felt overwhelming and even unattainable. In truth, I had carried an umbrella in anticipation of rain for so long that I did not know how to find the sun. For me, this was the most challenging hurdle to overcome. I had always been a problem solver, and up until this moment, had been able find the answer or the way out. This time, however, I was truly lost. It was a dark time in my life, but it also was a time of self-reflection and growth. I realized that in order to rebuild, I had to completely deconstruct the person and life I once knew. I proceeded to take a very hard and close look at my life, reevaluating my priorities, people, and plans.

I started with the simplest thing that I could think of. I began to listen to my body and try to give it what it needed to heal, and ultimately become stronger. I radically altered my diet, increased my amount of rest, and traded frequent, strenuous exercise for an active lifestyle. I think cancer forced me to slow down long enough to see that what I do in life should be things I truly enjoy, not things that I do because I am following the latest diet or exercise regimen. When I first started chemotherapy, I was determined to continue running. I felt that if I stopped I would somehow lose the person I knew, but halfway through treatment, a near fainting spell left me with no other choice than to give up the only sport I had ever known. Once I regained my strength, I decided on a slower pace of life. So with significant hesitation, I chose to permanently hang up my running shoes. I began the simple act of walking. During these walks, I began to see the world around me, and I eventually found the person I had been running from.
Another significant change I made was to increase the time I spent resting and sleeping. Before I became ill, I would set an alarm clock each day to make sure I could squeeze everything

into my day and fully complete each task on my never ending list. After I began treatment, I started sleeping in. At first, I slept in because my body simply would not get up, but later because it provided me with increased energy and mental clarity. One of my most transformative moments was likely when I stopped saying yes to everything, and started saying yes to fewer, but more important things. My decision was completely life changing, and I was amazed at the fact that it provided me the space to be fully present in my life, that, up until that time, I had lived but rarely seen.

One of the crucial components of my transformation was the decision to explore alternative treatments. They included a radical change in diet, mindfulness based practices, supplemental nutrients, and acupuncture. Before the diagnosis of cancer, I would have likely run in the opposite direction if offered to sit in complete silence, with only my own breath to keep me company. Furthermore, I would have laughed at the idea of acupuncture and cringed at the thought of drinking my vegetables. Thankfully, desperate times called for desperate measures, and so I willingly entered into the world of holistic treatment. This open-minded approach proved to be one of the smartest and most influential decisions of my life. It has not only provided me with a sense of control over my illness, but also has permanently altered my view of health and wellness.

True and viable answers come out of darkness. During the lowest point in my treatment process, I discovered my fear of cancer was not really a fear of the illness, but instead a fear of my own body taking me from the ones I held so dear. Also, I was acutely aware that I alone had to uncover my path to recovery, and that the same body and mind that had initially betrayed me, also held the key to my continued existence. At the time of diagnosis and treatment, I became a sponge, absorbing everything that was related to sustainable remission, but I was unclear as to what to do with this information. I entered into survival mode. Robotically, I would analyze overwhelming amounts of information floating around in my head, and I had to continuously fight the urge to become completely consumed by the world of cancer. One day during these dark hours, I decided that I needed to do exactly what I had told countless patients to do over the years. I had to break things into more manageable parts and meet each part head on. I made lists, charts, and mental road maps of each stage of my battle. In stopping, slowing down, and reprioritizing, I was able to obtain a clearer picture of what I needed to do to ultimately fight this illness and regain control of my life.

Most doctors and individuals describing the cancer process include the word "recovery". So when was the moment I finally celebrated my recovery? I think that the only way to answer this is to say that I have never recovered. At times I am still haunted by what I went through with cancer, realizing that this illness will always be an undeniable part of who I am. Therefore, I think that instead of using the words "recovered from an illness," to describe myself, I instead use the term "overcame an illness," To me, the word *recovered* suggests something has happened to us, that we lacked control as to when it arrived and when it finally departs. "Overcame an illness," proposes that we have bravely fought a battle. To stake a claim in the lives we want to lead and that ultimately we retain the ability to live despite our moments of illness or trauma. I have earned a place within my new life, one I took for granted, underappreciating its true fragility, and those that walked beside me down this road. Although I still have moments when I have to intentionally stop and focus on what is really important, I believe that I have finally found the secret to a happy life.

Great confusion and uncertainty typically follow when an individual has experienced a traumatic event. Ultimately, I took pre-calculated and carefully planned steps in order to claim my new life. Following my diagnosis, I closely examined what I had historically used to bury my hurt, pain, anxiety, and shame. From my self-evaluation, I realized I had used alcohol to disguise feelings of inadequacy and self-doubt. Although I would not have considered myself clinically addicted and rarely drank to the point of intoxication, I likely had become emotionally dependent on the numbing effect that alcohol provided. At times, I questioned my dependence, but I convinced myself that because I never drank during daylight hours, while attending to the needs of my children, or while at work, that I didn't have a problem. Since alcohol did not interrupt or affect my personal or professional life, nor did it prevent me from meeting goals or deadlines, I determined that I was just a social drinker like so many others I knew. Only after I stopped drinking entirely did I finally realize that alcohol not only fostered an emotional barrier in me, it also promoted for a pattern of increased anxiety. I drank to ease negative feelings of anxiety, but after the blocking of my emotions subsided, I was left with feelings of guilt and shame, creating a cycle of emotional dependency.

One doesn't have to do something every day, or in great amounts, to become dependent on it. One only needs to look to that thing to provide continued comfort and security that he or she feels cannot otherwise be achieved. I was not dependent on alcohol because a doctor told me that I was or because my professional or personal life was being affected. I felt that my dependency was linked to the emotional relief provided by this substance. Through research, I learned that hormone receptive cancer is known to be affected by certain amounts of alcohol; therefore, I made the immediate and life changing decision to stop drinking, or to at least greatly limit my alcohol intake. At times, this was a hard choice, since my decision occurred during a great time of stress. For many years, alcohol had provided me with a false sense of stress reduction. However, my determination to live proved to be much stronger than my need to drink, and so I exchanged alcohol for meditation, and began the process of trading other potentially unhealthy dependencies for life changing habits. Soon after this life change, I attended a party where, for the first time, I realized that I had the ability to remain present, engaged, and fully functional without alcohol. All I was missing was the dreaded morning hangover and enormous self-loathing! Amazingly, I did not miss the nighttime cocktails or the weekend parties. Instead, I woke up every morning feeling great, connected, and truly alive. Instead of half-heartedly connecting with my children and the amazing world around me because of being over served the prior night, I was able to continue to experience social gatherings and begin to celebrate the sun's rising each morning. Thanks to chemotherapy, I had spent six months with daily headaches and nausea, so the idea of purposefully providing for this self-torture was not something I eagerly embraced.

There are wake up calls, and then there calls that scream, "Pay attention, you idiot, this is your life passing you by!" I think that it's fair to say that I have experienced the latter. Throughout my battle with cancer, I asked the questions, "How are human resilience and strength measured? How do we determine how someone is handling a crisis, and when is it fair to say they are handling it well?" For the longest time, I thought that the fear of cancer was the thing that was so strong within me, but really it was never about cancer. What was strong within me was the need to live and the undeniable fear that something would take that away. At times during this journey, people would urge that I needed to remain positive, or that I needed to believe without a shadow of doubt that I would survive the ordeal. After listening to these statements, I would feel defeat or shame, as at times I feared my body would ultimately succumb to the effects of the illness. There were moments when I would compare myself to others, posing the question: "was I as strong as someone else?" but I ultimately realized that my survival was not dependent on how I measured up to everyone else. If anything, it was dependent on how I measured up to myself. I eventually learned that a piece of my being did not survive this war, but the components of myself that continued to thrive grew stronger and eventually became the core of who I am today.

When the clouds finally break, the sun peeks through, warming a damp and cold body in less than one minute. It is in that glorious moment that we realize that we are now standing in the sun. It's not clear the exact moment I claimed my own place in the sun, but what is extremely significant is the simple fact that I didn't wait for the sun to rise above me. Instead, I sought out the small spaces where the rays of warmth meet the frozen ground. The act of coming out of the darkness and claiming my place in the light meant fully embracing my life and the true meaning of this four-letter word. Prior to my diagnosis, I did not comprehend or respect the power and fragility of life, often taking for granted simple pleasures and moments. My battle would lead me to live a more purposeful life.

When I began the long battle to conquer cancer, I simultaneously entered into a struggle for a stronger sense of self. I quickly learned that the words "deconstructing" and "rebuilding" would be crucial in, not only my continued physical existence, but in realizing a life worth living. I decided that I could no longer hide behind the emotional limitations of anxiety, low self-esteem, and fear of things I could not control. If I was to deserve my beautifully messy and complicated existence, I had to stake a claim on it, and fast. Therefore, as I began to research the best treatments for my type of cancer, I also evaluated the pieces of myself that made up the broken woman before me.

Throughout the journey, it became clear that in order to build a stronger version of myself, I had to complete an essential and difficult task. The time had come for me to thoroughly examine the components of myself that caused self-loathing and created deep-seeded insecurity. I had to come to terms with who I innately was and cease the fight to be who everyone else wanted me to be. With all of the courage I could muster, I began the long road to fight for my identity, while at the same time fighting for my life.

The path to conquering cancer and strengthening myself began with a time of intense investigation. During this period, I became aware of three undeniable components of my personality: compassion, anxiety, and need for consistency. All of these pieces proved to be both detrimental and life-saving. They served great purpose during my fight with cancer, resulting in self-advocacy, clear and concise research, and the ability to create and maintain essential relationships. However, these also were the characteristics that induced stress, heartbreak, and self-doubt. I firmly believe that the pieces of each of us that are most challenging and can push us to our limits, are also the ones that can, when necessary, give us strength and provide for ultimate survival.

As I gained self-awareness, I slowly began to sift through those parts of myself that I wanted to foster and strengthen, and those parts that I needed to weed out. I realized that my cancer was more than defective rogue cells. It also was made up of my insecurities, self-hate, and a lifetime of regret. As the chemo worked its way through my body, killing off unwanted cells, I took on the role of emotionally eliminating those elements that had been a source of suffocation to me for almost twenty years. The detoxification of my emotional, mental, and physical selves brought me to my knees, and then gave me the ability to rise and stand on firmer ground.

Not long after my transformational journey began, I realized that my ultimate goal was to live a life I could be proud of. Although there were things in my past that I wished I had done differently, there were also things of which I was very proud: my work, dedication to motherhood, and strong friendships. But something was still missing. I did not feel like I had found a way to strengthen my inner-self, which I would later realize, resided at the core of my personal peace and happiness. I had become the person that I needed to become, but had I become the person I was meant to be?

The path to self-actualization is not an easy one. We must be willing to let go of everything we once knew to be true to ourselves and open up to the person who waits, quietly undiscovered. Only after an in depth look into the deepest parts of my soul, could I emerge as a person reborn. I do not think it was a coincidence that my last day of chemotherapy occurred on my birthday. It was the day I originally came into the world, and the day I reentered it as a woman, so very different than I had ever been.

A sense of connection is crucial to both positive human development and emotional stability. During cancer treatments, I often felt disjointed, making those rare moments of connection so vital. It was during a post-chemo Friday card game, that I would receive a lifeline to the outside world. Our dearest friends, Kirsten and Chrystie, had come over for what Suzi and I thought to be a routine weekly visit. As the four of us sat down and prepared for what had become our new version of Friday night excitement, they proceeded to hand me a thick envelope, which contained a neatly folded letter. As I began reading the letter, Chrystie started videotaping me. My uncertainty about what she was doing quickly turned to pure amazement and shock. The envelope's beautifully written letter informed me that people I didn't even know had raised money so that I could attend the live event of my dreams, a Sarah McLachlan concert. This was my first, but certainly not last, encounter with the amazing charity, Front Row Foundation.

Music has a way of linking people to one another and the world around them, but it also has the great ability to forge a link to the emotions within ourselves, and forever ties us to our life's experiences. The music of Sarah McLachlan had long ago made its way into my life and was present during my most important moments, such as discovering my real identity, the loss of our unborn child, and the joy of raising our two beautiful daughters. It gave me great comfort and exhilaration to know that experiencing her concert during my cancer treatment would be yet another critical moment when her music would be both an inspiration and a lifeline. Front Row Foundation is a nonprofit organization, which helps individuals and their families during times of critical illness by sending them to the live event of their dreams. Not only are individuals afforded the opportunity to attend these amazing performances, but they are also transported in style, and my case was no different.

When the day of our trip arrived and the black limo drove up in the dark, early morning, I could feel the energy in the air, and the love packed into each and every detail of the trip. Suzi, Kirsten, Chrystie, and I giggled like schoolgirls as we headed toward the airport, awaiting our journey to Atlanta. I was truly amazed and humbled by the details of the whole trip. The hotel room was beautiful and larger than my kitchen, the food was handpicked and carefully planned, and time had been built into the schedule for resting, which I greatly appreciated. After a short tour of the city, we began our night, at what I consider to be one of my top favorite restaurants of all time, Ocean Prime. The staff was unbelievably attentive, knowledgeable, and so very giving.

I cried several times throughout the meal, as the taste of sweet decadence melted in my mouth. During this beautifully crafted dinner, I was not a cancer patient, but just a girl going to a fancy dinner. I felt alive and so loved. As the limo approached the entrance to the concert, several people craned their necks to see if Sarah McLachlan was riding inside. Much to their dismay, it was simply a fragile but strong woman with her amazing entourage. I had never sat in the front row of a concert, enjoyed the exhilaration of being face-to-face with my favorite artist, or relished in the idea that I was somehow a part of this magical night. As the music started and the sun began to set over this beautiful outdoor pavilion, I felt like the words were meant for me, and that the music and I were intertwined in a magical dance of life. I continued to take in the evening, as we made our way to our front row seats, where I could embrace the amazing performance in all its glory. Halfway through the concert, Sarah stopped and explained that, prior to her tour, she had invited individuals from each event to submit a request to join her on stage. As she read the names of the lucky recipients, I was completely surprised and heart-stoppingly exhilarated when Melissa and Suzi were announced! Later, as I remembered that very special night, the following thought crossed my mind: One year before I had been told that I was part of a small percentage of women under the age of forty who receive a breast cancer diagnosis, and on the night of my Front Row experience, I was one of a very small percentage of individuals that would ever sit on stage with the wildly talented Sarah McLachlan.

After the shock subsided, Suzi and I looked at one another and realized that our beautiful friend, along with the support of this wonderful organization, had orchestrated this moment. Tears began rolling down my cheeks as I stood up to claim my place on the stage of life. The image of me in a video from that night remains so strongly embedded in my memory. In it, my arms are held high in the signature Front Row pose, with the crowd visible behind me. The image is a clear and permanent reminder of the moment that I would finally fight my way from the back to the front row of my life.

As I continued to search for ways in which to increase my connections to other cancer survivors, and to grab on to whatever pieces of life I could, I ran across two other amazing organizations. First Descents is a nonprofit organization that works to send individuals facing cancer to physically and spiritually rewarding outdoor experiences. After my experience with Front Row Foundation, I didn't think my view of the world could not get any better, but I was wrong. During the height of my treatment, I received an email stating that my application for the opportunity to participate in a First Descents program had been accepted, and I would be joining numerous other cancer fighters and survivors on a one-week rock climbing adventure. Although I was scared of this upcoming journey, I knew that I needed to push myself further than I ever had, and that if I could fight my way through cancer, I could certainly live through the unknowns of the trip. Unfortunately, I experienced some health setbacks and was unable to accept the opportunity. I was heartbroken, but knew that it was the right decision.

Just as I was thinking that my story with First Descents had ended, the organization gave me the opportunity to attend an event the very next year. My adventure was to brave white water rapids in the mountains of Vermont. When First Descents' staff told me that the accommodations would be camping-style, I really didn't know what to expect. I pictured something similar to summer camp, but unless you consider gourmet chefs willing to prepare meals based on your personal menu and twenty-four hour emotional and physical support summer camp, you are wrong. I was happily incorrect in my assumptions. As I walked off the plane to meet the energetic and caring camp leaders with First Descents, I knew that this would be an adventure of lifetime. Looking forward to the opportunity to go back to a time of innocence and summer fun, I climbed into the back of the black SUV, and from that moment on I was known as TKO (Technical Knockout). On the ride to the beautifully sprawling mountain cabin, a leader explained that each camper is given a nickname that describes her personality. Suzi had long ago given me the title "Too Stubborn to Fail," but the name was clearly too long, so an equally defining name was given to me. The staff, although prepared to handle the unique challenges faced by cancer patients, treated us not like cancer patients, but individuals living their lives to the fullest.

For five days, with limited cell phone service, I lived in a house with people I had never met, kayaked on rapids I never could have dreamed of, and once again lived my life in the front row.

My relationship with Beyond Boobs began when I was in the depths of cancer treatment. I will never forget my first breast cancer retreat. It was mere days after a date with the Red Devil and although I was ill and clearly not fit for travel, I drove two hours to a place where I would find a sisterhood like no other. Beyond Boobs is a nonprofit organization that provides support and education to young women diagnosed with breast cancer. This group of ladies became both my touchstone and an integral part of my family. Not only did I fully embrace this army of brave women, I eventually decided to become a volunteer facilitator for my local chapter. My connection to these women goes beyond cancer. I need these ladies as fish need water. The brave individuals of Beyond Boobs have shown me that I will never walk alone.

I credit these three organizations with not only helping me find my way out of the dark, but also finding my way to a stronger and healthier version of myself. The lessons that I learned and the memories that I made will last a lifetime, and will continue to shape my future. I make monthly donations to both First Descents and Front Row, and although I may never meet the individual recipients that benefit from my gifts, I know that even if it is small, I am making a difference in other people's lives. Isn't this why we are all here? To remain connected to one another, carry each other when we can no longer walk, and be the light in someone else's dark?

CHAPTER 7
A Guide to Thrive

Online Health Journal Entry

The Finish Line
Sep 22, 2014 11:11am

It is hard to believe that I have not posted something here since March, but I guess I have been busy living. :) As most of you already know, I had to stop taking the drug trial medication due to complications with my heart. I will continue to take a medication that will protect my heart for the next 6 months, but beyond that there does not seem to be any permanent damage. My hair has grown back and for the first time in my life, except for home perms, it has body. After taking some time off from work, I am back part-time which is exactly where I should be at this point. I honestly believe that our family has begun healing and that we are actually much stronger than we were when we started this journey. After a 12-week period of daily headaches, I elected to have some tests run, and I am so unbelievably happy to report that I am officially cancer free. Finally, we will soon be cheering Suzi on as she fulfills her lifetime dream of becoming a Hawaiian Ironman.

After much thought, oh who am I kidding, I always knew what I would do, I decided to have my ovaries removed. For some women, this procedure can decrease the chances of the cancer returning and it truly seemed like the right fit for my situation. So as I sit and recover from what I considered a walk in the park in comparison to last year, I have realized that, with the exception of a possible elective procedure in the future, my cancer journey has come to an end and I have crossed the finish line.

So what have I learned in the last year? I was telling Suzi just this morning that I too have trained for, and completed an Ironman. I have swum in the rough waters where there were times when I did not know if I would drown. I have ridden through the lava fields facing winds that were determined to keep me from moving forward. I have faced the roads of uncertainty and at times solitude. What I can say about completing the most important race of my life is that I am forever changed, and I will never look at life the same way again. I have learned that the people in your life that are there when you fall apart are the most amazing people you will ever meet, and you should hold tightly to them and never forget to tell them how much they mean. I have learned that no one is perfect, that we will all make mistakes, hurt others, hurt ourselves, and fail many times, but when all is said and done, what matters is that we get back on our feet or crawl in order to finish the race of life. I have learned that work, housekeeping, laundry, and yard work can wait, but happiness and peace is something that one must grab whenever the opportunity presents itself. I have learned that Suzi is my best friend. Not because we are the same

- I do not think there could be two more different souls - but because she has chosen to walk beside me even with my faults. I have learned that my family is strong and fierce, and I am not just speaking of my immediate family. I am also speaking of my family of origin, my family of marriage, and my family of choice. Finally, I have learned that I am amazingly lucky to have been given this life. One day as I was waiting for my test results to come back, I prayed, but I did not just pray for clear results. Instead, I prayed for the chance to be a better version of myself. I want to be a more patient mother, a more loving and appreciative partner, a more devoted friend, and to have the ability to continue to help others and make a difference in this world. I think that in the end all we can strive for is the strength and wisdom to continue to be stronger and healthier versions of the wonderful people who already exist.

My dear friend Anne and I often say that having one another as a sounding board is crucial, and we often try to limit discussions of cancer to one another so that we do not overburden others. We would typically hold these conversations during our routine walks, but one unusually warm spring day our talk took a surprising turn. Although started by catching up on the latest cancer stories, we spent most of our time talking about her work or future events. The key word here is future. You see Anne and I have spent the better part of a year living day to day or rather doctors' appointment to doctors' appointment, and today we talked about the future - a future without cancer. As Anne and I rounded the corner to her house while discussing her upcoming home renovation, I realized that we had crossed the finish line just as we started the race...together. Here is to you my friend and to all of the other individuals that have walked, run, or crawled down this road where uncertainty, inspiration, pain, peace, and true bravery can always be found.

Love to All,
M

There were days when the never-ending presence of my illness wrapped me in a blanket of sorrow and loss. But I had to go on, if not for myself, then for those who walked the path with me, and for those before me who had bravely fought cancer. So I kept trying, determined to once again feel the sun on my face, if only for a week, day, hour, or minute. Experiencing great tragedy taught me a great deal, but the most important thing was that in order to thrive, I would need three things: **a new perspective, compassion for myself, and a sense of purpose.**

What does self-care look like in the midst of tragedy? When great devastation and loss occur, how to we find strength and courage to fight, not only for our continued existence, but for the opportunity to pick up the fragments of our lives and build a more resilient sense of self? For me, the answers to these questions were as important to my survival as the chemotherapy that flowed through my veins. I believed that in order to transform tragedy into a life I could be proud of, I would first need to create a stronger sense of who I was at my very core, and who I ultimately wanted to become. Right now you might be asking the question, "How can I take care of myself when I feel lost, broken, and hopeless?" It isn't easy, and I guarantee there will be moments when you do not know how to go on.

Following times of anger, fear, and sadness, we discover our great capacity for healing. We learn that if we can survive these dark hours and days, we can actually strengthen our ability to forgive, be fearless, and find happiness. Self-care and compassion will be the land where you choose to build your transformed life. If you do not take time to care for your living, breathing self, then this reclaimed life will crumble to the ground. Expressing both positive and challenging feelings is an important demonstration of our continued connection to the world. There are a many ways to release emotions including, but not limited to: journaling, art, exercise, prayer, meditation, or participating in a support group. Find the method that works for you. Take time out of each day to do something positive for yourself, even if it's small.

Make sure it is an activity that you truly enjoy, and provides you with contentment and comfort. Keep in mind that these techniques may only work for a period of time, or it might take awhile for them to take hold. Keep trying, because trying is moving and if we are still moving, we are still here. Remember the first time you tried to ride a bike, and you felt as though you would topple over at any moment? The feeling of flying and the fear of crashing happening simultaneously within your heart? This is what a life transformation feels like. It is the freedom that comes with letting go and the fear of this reckless abandonment that makes this journey both exciting and terrifying.

Self-care and compassion are two of the most crucial components of the transformation process. Another crucial step in the process of reconstruction is research. This practice will be the key to uncovering the building blocks with which to build your transformed life, so it is essential that you take time and energy to pick the right materials. I recommend obtaining a journal where you can keep track of all of the information you are gathering, as it can all be overwhelming and confusing. Also, it is important to weed out information that is not beneficial or is damaging. For example, when I first began my research related to prevention of reoccurrence, I found hundreds of websites and thousands of opinions. At times, the information I discovered increased my anxiety or produced unnecessary fear, which was harmful. Since I was in a period of absorbing all that I could find, even the tiniest thread of information could send me spinning. I remember once when I was looking up information related to my specific pathology report, everything that I found indicated that my chances of survival were compromised due to the aggressive nature of my tumor, my lymph node involvement, and even my age. Of course there was also information out there that would say that I had greater chances of remission, so I really never knew what to believe and how to feel.

When gathering information, it is important to research articles and other sources related to beneficial coping mechanisms, overall health, grief and loss, but also take time to research the most essential piece of the puzzle - you. I spent hours, and sometimes weeks, gathering information regarding the latest treatments, the best ways to eat, and the importance of reducing outside stress. I found that I could do every single one of those external things, but if I didn't close my eyes and sit with my own thoughts, feelings, and needs, then the rest of my efforts were worthless. In the deepest parts of my body, I knew that if I was going to walk in the land of the living, I had to somehow become whole again. I was the only one that could make it happen. During this time, I discovered that I was no longer afraid to be alone, and that I could be my biggest advocate and become so much more than I ever thought possible. I also learned that, from the moment of diagnosis, I was a cancer survivor, and was now doing the work to earn the much-coveted title of *cancer thriver*. My realization didn't occur without a fight, as it followed a time of great despair.

After my miscarriage, part of me did not want to go on. During cancer treatment, I had the same feelings. The body chills came, and I felt like I was a puzzle with so many pieces missing, that no one could make out what image the pieces were supposed to create. I know I am not alone in these feelings, and I want you to know that you are not alone either. What gave me the will to go on? Honestly, the main thing was that I did not want my children or Suzi to go through what my family went through when my father died, creating deep wounds that took many years to heal. Secondly, I felt that I needed to help others who did not have the support that I had, or individuals who were struggling and felt alone and lost. I decided that I had to find a greater purpose, something I continue to cling to today. My reasons for living are ever evolving, and although I know that tomorrow is not guaranteed, I feel that continuing to connect to this world and those in it are critical to my ability to thrive. Finally, during my time of self-exploration, I discovered that what I have always wanted to do was to inspire others. By providing people with hope, they could be motivated to keep going even if it is for just one minute at a time. I made the decision that if I were going to be here on Earth without breasts and with an uncertain future, I would not waste the time I had been given. Instead I would become amazing.

How do we find purpose during a time when we are struggling to find reasons to get out of bed each day, and reenter the life that has ultimately betrayed our innocence? Ultimately, we have to change our perspective. Our vision of how our life should be is similar to the rooms within a reconstructed home. We have the ability to decide how these rooms will look, and more importantly, what we will use them for. There are only a handful of things that are guaranteed in this world. Two of them, life and death, have no specified time frame, so our perception related to human existence is the first thing that we must reconstruct. For me, this important step has been both challenging and panic inducing. The idea that, even with all that I have done to increase my chances of living a long life, there is still no guarantee, will often cause me to lose my breath and leave me emotionally paralyzed. Death is an inescapable part of the journey that we are on, so we have to choose to not just live but to be alive! I cannot stress this enough, and will continue to refer to it whenever I get caught up in the fast-paced world. As an example, before cancer I believed I was professionally successful, and to the outside observer it was true. In reality, I was overscheduled and had little space or time in my days to think. I was always running, trying to catch up.

Since being diagnosed with breast cancer, I have turned three life-long dreams into realities. I've written a book, become an inspirational speaker, and worked with social work students at the college level. None of these would have been possible had I not stopped to ask myself, "What inspires me? What is my purpose in life?" I took the time to sit in the rooms of my reconstructed house, learning what the rooms wanted to become. Only after I had thrown out all of the things that took up precious space in them could I make room for those things that were waiting to shine.

Approximately two years after my initial surgery, I found out that a friend had recently been diagnosed with breast cancer. Knowing very well the road that was in front of her, I immediately signed up to be a part of her support crew. One day after she and I had met to discuss treatment options and upcoming obstacles, I drove away and a familiar feeling began creeping in. One I instantly recognized as the heaviness and overwhelming nature of breast cancer. As the feeling grew, I prepared myself for several days of sadness and worry. I drove by a church in my neighborhood where they were hosting their weekly food pantry. I stopped the car, turned it around, and sat outside of the church, not sure if I could make myself go in to interact with others. Much to my surprise, I went inside, where I lost myself, not in my own sorrow, but in connecting with and helping others. I had spent almost twenty years as a social worker, convinced that the work that I was doing was of value. I was helping others and making a difference, but I always knew I could do more.

The realization did not send me out searching for additional jobs or professional responsibilities. Instead, it led me to redefine what being a social worker meant to me, and to deepen the work I did with others. Before my illness, my professional and personal success revolved around the concept of quantity. How many individuals could I reach? How much time was I spending with my kids? How many miles did I run? Now my life is based on the idea of quality. I focus my attention on different questions: How can I best contribute to the well-being of others? How can I provide my children with the best parts of myself? What have I learned of myself and this life that I have been given?

The journey out of darkness is challenging at best, and there is not a right or wrong way to move away from sorrow and grief and toward a reconstructed self. We are only experimenters in this thing we call life, constantly taking chances, making mistakes, and hopefully stumbling across a theory that will contribute to personal growth and the ability to thrive. Am I scared that cancer will return? Do I wish that I could go back in time when my innocence was intact? The answers are complicated. There are many days when I am afraid that this illness will eventually take me away from my children, but I have realized that the innocence I speak of was imagined, and never truly existed. I was under the misguided impression that the opportunity to see my children grow was a given, and that time was immeasurable. I see now that I was wrong. The beautiful fragility of life, and the truth that my time will end at some point, is the place where innocence lives. For example, when we lose someone, our love for them actually intensifies. Or, if we are told that we only have months to live, we spend our time actually living the life we had always planned but never stopped to experience. We cannot replace the things we have lost. As much as we yearn for the touch of a deceased loved one, the days when cancer was something we only read about in books, or divorce was a thing that other people went through, this is our truth, reality, and a permanent piece of our puzzle. Standing up and taking back your life in no way means that you have not suffered or that you are leaving someone or something behind. It does mean that, just as flowers can grow amongst rubble and destruction, so too can your life **emerge triumphant.**

34288269R00054

Made in the USA
Middletown, DE
17 August 2016